THE AMERICAN SOLDIER

FROM THE CIVIL WAR TO THE WAR IN IRAQ

THE AMERICAN SOLDIER

FROM THE CIVIL WAR TO THE WAR IN IRAQ

A PHOTOGRAPHIC TRIBUTE

Edited by
CYMA RUBIN

Foreword by
DAVID DOUGLAS DUNCAN

BUSINESS of ENTERTAINMENT Inc.
New York

THE AMERICAN SOLDIER
FROM THE CIVIL WAR TO THE WAR IN IRAQ
A Photographic Tribute

Presented by
Cyma Rubin, President
Business Of Entertainment Inc.
347 Fifth Avenue
New York, NY 10016
www.bizzent.org

ACKNOWLEDGMENTS

EXHIBITION CATALOG

DESIGNER
Jay Anning, Thumb Print

HISTORICAL TEXT
Gary Helm Darden, Ph.D.
Fairleigh Dickinson University

ARTS AND HUMANITIES RESOURCES
Kathrine Walker Schlageck, Senior Educator,
and Lorne Render, Director,
Marianna Kistler Beach Museum of Art
Kansas State University

EDITORIAL ADVISER
James Waller, Thumb Print

The exhibition catalog is sponsored by
John B. Stetson Company

STETSON®
AN AMERICAN SPIRIT

Foreword excerpted from *This is War!* by David Douglas
Duncan (New York: Harper Bros., 1951). Used by permission.

Additional photo credits:
Page 2: Will Dickey/*Florida Times Union*
Pages 6–7: John Gaps III/The Associated Press
Page 8: Courtesy David Douglas Duncan Photography
Collection, Harry Ransom Humanities Research Center,
University of Texas at Austin

EXHIBITION

CURATOR
Cyma Rubin

DESIGNER
Kenneth Foy

PHOTO CONSULTANT
Hal Buell

PROJECT MANAGER
Joseph White

The exhibition is sponsored by

EADS
NORTH AMERICA

BUSINESS of
ENTERTAINMENT Inc.

Library of Congress Control Number: 2007908717

ISBN: 978-0-615-17321-4

Printed and bound in China

10 9 8 7 6 5 4 3 2 1

This catalog and the photographic exhibition on which it is based are a tribute to the American soldier—to all the men and women who join the military because they proudly want to serve their country. When there is peace, their readiness is the backbone of our security. In battle, they fight and die for us.

The photographs collected here include images ranging from the bloody Civil War clashes fought in our nation's heartland to present-day battles in the streets of Baghdad. Their focus is on the soldiers themselves—those who march the dusty trails, climb the icy ridges, dig the muddy trenches, carve paths through the jungle, and endure the blinding sandstorms, the treacherous heat and cold, and the constant discomfort of life at the front. They know the face of the enemy and the hellfire of war.

Since photography's birth more than 150 years ago, the camera has become the soldier's historical notebook. As photography improved, the camera got closer and closer to the soldiers' lives, capturing the hard times, the humor, the bravery, the camaraderie, the victories, and, sometimes, the ultimate sacrifice—death. Like the soldiers themselves, war photographers have risked their lives to record moments that change history and forever impact our lives.

I hope these pages will bring the reader closer to an understanding of the American soldier, so that when they see soldiers, they will see more than just the uniforms . . . they will see these young men and women as the courageous human beings they are.

Cyma Rubin
Curator/Editor

THIS IS WAR!

This is an effort to completely divorce the word "war," as flung dramatically down off the highest benches of every land, from the look in the man's eyes who is taking his last puff on perhaps his last cigarette, perhaps forever, before he grabs his rifle, his guts and his dreams—and attacks an enemy position above him. There is neither climax nor ringing conclusion. It is simply an effort to show something of what a man endures when his country decides to go to war, with or without his personal agreement on the righteousness of the cause.

The photographs here reflect only what the men did, something of what they felt, and probably very little of what they thought. Yet, to learn their stories, each photograph must be read as carefully as you might read a page of written text in a novel. Asking you to read the story in their faces and hands and bodies, as they were feeling it themselves at the moment of impact, is only fair to them.

As a war photographer, I wanted to show what war did to a man. I wanted to show something of the comradeship that binds men together when they are fighting a common peril. I wanted to show the way men live and die, when they know Death is among them, and yet they still find the strength to crawl forward only with bayonets to stop the advance of men they have never seen, with whom they have no immediate quarrel, men who will kill them on sight if given first chance. I wanted to show something of the agony, the suffering, the terrible confusion, the heroism which is everyday currency among those men who actually pull the triggers of rifles aimed at other men known as "the enemy." I wanted to tell a story of war, as war has always been for men through the ages. Only their weapons, the terrain, the causes have changed.

D.D.D.
March 1951

It's the same, today.

David Douglas Duncan
23 July 2007

CIVIL WAR
1861 - 1865

I can't tell you how funny I feel knowing tomorrow I'll see a big battle. Kind of scared inside but I'm not going to run.

> —Private John C. Davis, writing from
> Gettysburg, July 2, 1863
>
> (Private Davis was killed the next day. He was 14 years old.)

The Civil War remains by far the deadliest war in U.S. history. Over its four years, more than 600,000 Union and Confederate soldiers perished of wounds and disease before the North could compel the South's surrender in April 1865. The estimated cost of the war for both sides exceeded $20 billion.

Although the issue of slavery was foremost among the Civil War's causes, the question that directly led to the eruption of hostilities was not whether slavery itself should survive but whether it should be allowed in the Western territories acquired by the United States after the Mexican-American War. The last tether of political compromise between the free states of the North and the slave states of the South was lost in the presidential election of November 1860, when Abraham Lincoln won on a platform prohibiting the spread of slavery.

For seven states in the Deep South, Lincoln's victory was intolerable. By February 1861, they had seceded from the Union and formed the Confederate States of America. In his inaugural address in March, the new president vowed to defend the Union and to protect federal forts in the South. In April, the Confederate army bombarded Fort Sumter in Charleston, South Carolina. Four states in the Upper South soon voted for secession and likewise joined the Confederacy.

Generations of political negotiation had finally given way to military struggle. As one Union private wrote to his sister in April 1862, "Truly we know not the horrors of war till peace has fled." Five months later he was killed. Each side had to mobilize huge numbers of men to fight a protracted war, and military service dramatically altered the lives of millions of citizen soldiers.

Men of Company M, 3rd Rhode Island Artillery, put two 100-pounder Parrott rifles into action, firing on Fort Sumter, South Carolina, from nearby Morris Island, 1863.
Haas and Peale

The glory of war was often lost on these enlisted men, who dearly missed the comforts of life at home. Suddenly, they were forced to march countless miles, to sleep on the ground in all weather, and to endure not being able to bathe or wash their clothes—and to suffer the lice infestations that resulted. The quality of their food was poor, and the water they drank was often contaminated—so often that an estimated 57,000 soldiers died from water-borne illnesses alone. Above all, these men had to obey orders in the heat of battle—and to kill other men who until very recently had been their compatriots. Bloody and costly, the Civil War was also terribly emotionally wrenching.

It was also vastly more lethal than earlier conflicts. The smoothbore muskets used in previous wars had not been accurate at distances greater than eighty yards, requiring close

proximity in battle. But new rifle technology featuring spiraled grooves inside the gun barrel gave the new, conical bullets a spin, increasing shooters' precision and reach. Now, a rifleman could strike an enemy from a position up to a thousand yards away.

Despite these advances in weaponry, officers on both sides were slow to adjust their tactics, continuing to believe that tight drill formations were necessary for concentrating rapid firepower. But these formations also created concentrated targets—and concentrated casualties. And the soft-lead bullets caused terrible wounds that proved difficult to heal, often leading to gangrene and limb amputation.

American soldiers were, in fact, fighting a brand-new kind of war, and the mounting numbers of dead and wounded on both sides bore testimony to its grim realities. When

A rare photo of a Union Army Women's Volunteer Unit visiting Washington, D.C. Women who volunteered during the Civil War represented different social levels and backgrounds, from debutante to prostitute.

National Archives

nearly 100,000 soldiers clashed at Shiloh in April 1862, the casualties from this single two-day battle were greater than all American losses during the Revolutionary War, the War of 1812, and the Mexican-American War combined. The Battle of Gettysburg, in July 1863, would outstrip even that carnage. In the largest battle ever waged in North America, more than 160,000 soldiers fought for three days, sustaining 51,000 casualties. "I have been over other battlefields but never one like this," wrote one Union private to his fiancée. "In one place I counted 16 [corpses] in a spot no larger than your kitchen. It was a hard sight."

At the outset of the war, medical care and hospital facilities were primitive. The Army Medical Corps began with just 87 men. Regimental hospitals were usually quartered in tents. If a battle was in play, an "advance" station (or dressing station) was set up behind the battle lines. The wounded either walked or were carried by stretcher-bearers to the station, where they were given a stout drink of liquor and an opium pill; morphine was rubbed into their wounds. The field hospital itself (which might be in a farmhouse, school, or church) was usually five miles from enemy artillery. The wounded lay on the bare ground awaiting their turn on the operating table. Amputation was the order of the day.

By 1862, both armies had developed larger and better field hospitals. The surgical staffs were improved, and female nurses, who proved very popular with the soldiers, replaced many of the untrained male nurses. After treatment, the wounded were evacuated by railroad and riverboats to general hospitals. The hospitals also became cleaner, and the food improved as matrons took over the supervision of the kitchens. By the time the war ended, more than 11,000 doctors had served.

Although the Civil War began with all-volunteer forces, the escalating demand for more and more troops led to the use of conscription by both North and South—the first military drafts in American history. The Confederacy passed its first conscription law in April 1862, and the Union turned to conscription a year later, with registration triggering a violent riot in New York City in July 1863. Exemptions in the North and South for those who could afford to purchase a replacement inspired widespread—and legitimate— charges of class discrimination.

The Civil War also brought African Americans into military service to an unprecedented degree. Desperation led the South, during the final weeks of war, to form several companies of slave soldiers—though it was by then too late for them to see battle. The Union, on the other hand, had passed its first law allowing African Americans to enlist as early as July 1862. Ultimately, 180,000 black soldiers would serve in the Union army—fully 10 percent of its ranks. They engaged in combat as early as October 1862 and, except for Sherman's invasion of Georgia, served in every major campaign in 1864–1865. An estimated one-third of all African-American troops lost their lives for the Union cause. Sixteen won the Congressional Medal of Honor.

Sgt. James H. Harris poses with the Medal of Honor he was awarded for "gallantry in the assault" on Chaffin's Farm, Virginia, September 29, 1864.
Library of Congress

Once slaves, these men joined the Union Army. By the end of the war, 180,000 African Americans had fought for their freedom.
Library of Congress

*At an overcrowded Union field hospital at Savage Station, Virginia, soldiers rest after
primitive treatment following a battle on June 27, 1862.*

James F. Gibson

Teenager Jackson, a former slave and drummer for the Union Army, was in the 78th U.S. Colored Infantry.
National Archives

Pvt. Gustave Schumann, a teenager, was bugler for the 40th Regiment of New York State's Volunteer Infantry.
U.S. Army

Some families accompanied the men to camps. At the 31st Pennsylvania Infantry camp near Washington, D.C., a woman, children, and a man who may be her husband pose for the photographer.
Library of Congress

Beyond the traditional burden of tending the home fires while men were off fighting, an estimated 400 women served in battle units during the war, also performing as nurses, spies, and scouts. From every class they followed husbands and lovers into war, often in male disguise, and endured hardships that many thought impossible for women to bear. Many such women earned the respect of male soldiers even as a few rose to become sergeants, even officers. It is estimated that more than 60 women were wounded or killed in Civil War battles. After the Battle of Gettysburg, the bodies of two uniformed Confederate soldiers were found to be women, while the remains of a Union flag bearer in uniform were also female.

In early 1865, after four weary years of fighting, the Confederate army was low on manpower and supplies against a Union army twice its size. That spring, the Army of the Confederacy, reduced to fewer than 30,000 men, abandoned the Southern capital of Richmond and retreated deeper into Virginia. On April 9, its commander, General Robert E. Lee, surrendered to Union general Ulysses S. Grant at Appomattox Court House. Five days later, President Lincoln, whose election triggered the war, was assassinated.

A Southern battery takes up its position during a drill near Ringgold, Georgia.
Mathew Brady

The war was over, and it was time for hundreds of thousands of soldiers to go back home. Union troops, buoyed by victory, were greeted with grand parades and awarded the first veterans' pension in American history. For Confederate soldiers, the return journey was far bleaker, as they traveled through a ruined landscape of destroyed homes and ravaged farms. The Union had been saved, but the veterans on both sides would contest the meaning and memory of the Civil War for decades to come.

"California Joe," who was billed as one of the North's deadliest sharpshooters.
Courtesy Vermont Historical Society

An embalming surgeon prepares a soldier's body for shipment home for burial.
Library of Congress

A dead Confederate soldier lies in a crude defensive trench at the siege of Petersburg, Virginia, April 3, 1865.
Library of Congress

A violent battle shattered Antietam, Maryland, leaving behind this scene of death and destruction in front of Dunker Church.
Alexander Gardner

AMERICAN SOLDIERS ON FOREIGN SOIL
1898 - 1902

This war is something terrible. You see sights you could hardly believe, and a life is hardly worth a thought.
—Charles R. Wyland, Washington State Volunteers, writing from the Philippines, March 27, 1899

Few Americans celebrating the New Year in 1898 could have imagined that by 1900 an army of tens of thousands of American troops would be enmeshed in an insurgent guerilla war in the Philippine Islands. The archipelago, situated in the strategic heart of East Asia, had been a Spanish colony since 1565. Yet the 1898 Treaty of Paris that ended the Spanish-American War marked the demise of the Spanish Empire in both the Caribbean and the Pacific. For the sum of $20 million, the United States gained custody of Guam, Puerto Rico, and the Philippines—a tropical landmass the size of Arizona scattered across more than 7,000 islands, and with nearly 8 million inhabitants. Cuba, meanwhile, became a semi-independent U.S. protectorate.

The "Splendid Little War," as Secretary of State John Hay called the Spanish-American conflict, lasted only a few months. But it was just the opening salvo in a series of engagements. The half-decade that followed the 1898 war ushered in a new set of strategic objectives that American soldiers would fight to uphold—doing so far beyond the shores of North America.

Soldiers of the 17th Infantry head to the front in the Philippines in 1900 to fight an insurgency that would last until just before the start of World War I.
B.W. Kilburn

A recruiting station on the streets of New York City signs up volunteers for a modernized U.S. Army, soon to be involved in struggles on foreign soil.
Courtesy Corbis

Following the end of the Civil War, the primary focus of U.S. military effort had been the American West, with the army playing a crucial role as the nation consolidated its hold on the vast territories stretching from the Great Plains to the Pacific. Here, the primary theater of battle for American soldiers was against a few hundred thousand Native Americans who resisted expansion into their ancestral lands. The decades-long series of Indian Wars ended only with the Indians' final military defeat in 1890 and their relocation to federal reservations. The closing of this chapter in American history coincided, the same year, with what the U.S. Census Bureau called the "closing of the frontier"—the loss of contiguous land for new settlement, which had defined American expansion ever since English colonists settled along the Atlantic coast in the early 17th century.

Beginning in 1898, the geographic focus of U.S. expansion shifted, becoming a global front in which the American soldier would fight in three key conflicts in five years. The first—the unilateral war against a Spanish empire weighed down by independence revolutions in Cuba and the Philippines—lasted just 16 weeks. The prosecution of the Spanish-American War required an unprecedented coordination of U.S. armed forces and

New recruits take the oath at a training camp at Niagara Falls, New York. Troops were prepared for coming encounters in Cuba, Puerto Rico, the Philippines, and China.
M.H. Zahner

relied on the U.S. navy to deploy Marines and army troops in multiple island theaters. Shots were fired from the Philippines and Guam in the Pacific to Cuba and Puerto Rico in the Caribbean. The most decisive ground operations were in Cuba, where the Spanish had their largest forces. But with its navy soon destroyed and its colonies cut off from reinforcements, Spain sued for peace. Little more than 300,000 Americans served in the armed forces during the war, and, by the standards of the day, a modest 2,000 died (just 385 in battle). Nearly 1,700 others were wounded.

In this and subsequent conflicts, U.S. army regulars had the advantage of superior weapons, namely the Krag-Jørgensen five-shot, bolt-action rifle. Adopted by the army in 1892, the Norwegian-designed, American-made, .30 caliber rifle offered the first smokeless powder round for the American soldier. But with too few Krags for the army's

American soldiers land at Baiguiri, Cuba, to combat Spain's defense of Cuba, 1898.
Signal Corps

swollen ranks, many volunteer soldiers were issued the older, .45 caliber, single-shot Springfield rifles, whose smoke, emitted from firing, revealed their position to the enemy. Nonetheless, American soldiers in the field had the additional benefit of the most modern machine guns and breach-loading artillery, whereas their enemies often had a motley collection of older or captured weapons.

While the Spanish-American War helped mend the sectional divide between white Northerners and white Southerners, African Americans, too, played a valuable role. They had served in the U.S. army since the Civil War, after which Congress created all-black infantry and cavalry regiments. Over time, these units came to be known as the Buffalo Soldiers, so named by Native Americans during the Great Plains wars. Having served with distinction, primarily in the West, from 1866 through the early 1890s, the Buffalo Soldiers now saw combat in Cuba. More than two dozen black cavalrymen accompanied Lieutenant Colonel Theodore Roosevelt and his Rough Riders in their famous charge up San Juan Hill, while other Buffalo Soldiers helped secure Kettle Hill. Five African-American soldiers earned the Congressional Medal of Honor for valor during this war, and many went on to fight in the Philippine-American War.

With the peace treaty secured from Spain in December 1898, the United States sought to retain the Philippines as a U.S. territory—by force if necessary. But U.S. objectives for the region clashed with Philippine nationalist aspirations. When U.S. forces attempted to occupy the archipelago in February 1899, war broke out with the Philippine Nationalist Army. The U.S. military, however, was ill prepared for a sudden and sustained escalation of American power in multiple theaters overseas. The regular army possessed little more than 28,000 troops when the Spanish-American War began in April 1898. Congress hastily doubled the army's size, to nearly 57,000 men, while President William McKinley called on the states to muster 125,000 volunteers for a one-year enlistment. But many more would be needed in the Philippines when these enlistments ran out. By 1900, a U.S. force of 70,000 men was deployed in the Philippines.

Nor were these troops prepared for modern insurgent warfare in a tropical climate, which sapped their morale and fighting strength. The Philippine War, in fact, became the longest and most controversial U.S. war in the half-century between the Civil War and the United States' entry into World War I. Both sides publicized claims of atrocities, while the American public at home waged a heated debate on the merits of both the

Col. Theodore Roosevelt and his famed Rough Riders stand victorious atop San Juan Hill, Cuba, 1898.
William Dinwiddie

African-American soldiers train at Camp Wikoff, New York, before assignment to the Philippines, c. 1898.
Signal Corps

annexation and the war being fought to secure it. These issues were hardly lost on the American soldier: "Of course I feel pity for the dead and wounded," wrote one Oregon volunteer in 1899, "but it all adds to the general feeling of horror for the whole business of war. I wonder if people would have wanted these God-forsaken islands if they had foreseen the cost." A Colorado volunteer wrote of the war's impact on his fellow soldiers: "None of the men are the same as they left home, either physically or mentally, and the only thing that will do us any good is to get us home. Any one can have our share of these islands any time they let us get home."

Containing the insurgency was critical to the U.S. effort. U.S. navy gunboats brought supplies and reinforcements to the American fighting forces while naval blockades precluded foreign arms and supplies from reaching the nationalists—a powerful counterpoint to the absence of such support in the later wars in Vietnam and Iraq. Although localized fighting would continue in some islands for years, the United States declared the insurgency over on July 4, 1902. By then, 125,000 American soldiers had served in the Philippines. Of the 4,300 who died, at least two-thirds succumbed to disease. As one soldier from the 14th Regulars wrote, "I don't think there is a Spanish bullet made to kill me; it is disease that I am most afraid of." Another 2,800 American soldiers were wounded.

For the Philippine people, the cost was even more appalling. While upwards of 20,000 Philippine nationalist soldiers died, estimates place the number of Philippine civilian fatalities somewhere between 250,000 and 500,000, the vast majority due to famine and disease induced by the war. Despite the terrible human toll, the United

States achieved its strategic goal—the pacification of the Philippines and the islands' recognition of U.S. rule—in three and a half years. The Philippines would not receive full independence until 1946.

What lured the United States to possess the Philippines was, in part, what had lured the Spanish and other European powers into the region: proximity to the fabled China market. Covering an area larger than the United States and with more than four times its population, China promised the imperial powers both commercial and spiritual rewards. Foreign businessmen saw opportunities for trade and investment, while Catholic and Protestant missionaries perceived a new arena for making converts. In reality, however, the long-ruling Qing dynasty ruled over an impoverished peasant base still tied to subsistence agriculture. Moreover, 60 years of foreign invasions and domestic rebellions had destabilized China. During that time, the foreign powers had secured territorial spheres of influence throughout coastal China, granting themselves privileges that

U.S. Army Engineers carry out maneuvers in Cuba in preparation for battle with Spanish forces.
National Archives

◀ *American soldiers entrenched in the Philippines, ready to fire at the rebels, c. 1899–1900.*
B.W. Kilburn

▲ *Soldiers of the 9th Infantry take a break at their campsite in a courtyard at the Forbidden City in China.*
Library of Congress

exempted their nationals from Chinese law. Meanwhile, some 2,000 foreign missionaries had claimed the souls of nearly 800,000 converts; though these newly minted Christians represented just a fraction of 1 percent of the total population, many of them were also granted exemption from Chinese law because of their religious affiliation. These gains by foreign powers were often secured by the threat and show of force and owed much to the industrial powers' technological advantage in weapons and transportation.

By 1900 the domestic situation in China had reached a boiling point. The so-called Boxer rebels, named for their practice of Chinese shadowboxing, fomented discontent among the masses in northeastern China. With the tacit support of the Dowager Empress in the capital, Peking (now Beijing), they targeted sites of foreign influence. In the spring of 1900, they ripped up rail and telegraph lines and murdered foreign missionaries and many of their Chinese converts. The rebels then laid siege to the 85-acre walled compound in Peking that housed the official diplomatic missions and residences of 11 foreign powers. The siege lasted 55 days, during which the outside world had no knowledge of the fate of those imprisoned within the compound. Only the arrival of an international force of 20,000 troops saved them from certain death.

Among those troops were 2,500 American soldiers deployed from the Philippines—their presence signaling the third foreign conflict for the United States in this era. For the first time, American soldiers participated in a multilateral army outside North America, marching alongside soldiers from Great Britain, Russia, France, Germany, Austria, Italy, and Japan. It marked the shape of things to come for the American soldier in the turbulent 20th century, the most violent century in history.

Soldiers drill in China's Forbidden City, where U.S. forces helped to halt the Boxer Rebellion.
National Archives

WORLD WAR I
1914 - 1918

All the hills . . . have been fought over many times and the result is that they are in waves of dirt with one shell hole overlapping the next; no grass or anything growing; no trees but where there used to be a forest you can see some black spots where the roots remain.

> —Stull Holt, American Expeditionary Force, writing from France, September 1, 1917

Europe was at the zenith of its power when World War I broke out in August 1914. The magnitude of the carnage left eyewitnesses aghast. Of the more than 65 million men mobilized worldwide, at least 8.5 million were killed. In 51 straight months of warfare, an average of 5,500 were slaughtered every day! Added to this calamity were the more than 21 million deaths worldwide from the Spanish influenza pandemic of 1918–1919, whose rapid spread was abetted by the movement of troops. It is no wonder that, for a generation afterward, World War I was called the Great War.

Although the United States accounted for just over 2 percent of all Allied fatalities and waged war for little more than one-third of the war's duration, the Americans' 19 months of belligerence proved decisive. Not only did America's factories and fields provide the Allies with vital supplies, but the eventual presence of 2 million American soldiers in France tipped the scales to Allied victory.

Congestion on the roads at the rear of American lines kept vehicles from moving faster than two miles per hour in the Argonne Forest in France, 1918.
National Archives

World War I was caused by rabid nationalism in Europe, fed by a cutthroat race for colonies and markets. "The situation is extraordinary," wrote one envoy to President Woodrow Wilson before the war. "It is militarism run stark mad." Out of these circumstances emerged two rival camps: the principal Allies of Great Britain, France, Russia, and later Italy, and the chief Central Powers of Germany, Austria-Hungary, and later the Ottoman Empire. The assassination of the heir to the Austro-Hungarian throne in Sarajevo, Serbia, on June 28, 1914, lit the fuse that ignited World War I.

The war's most decisive theater was the Western Front, cutting 475 miles across France from the English Channel to the Alps. Here multimillion-man armies dug some 25,000 miles of trenches. The industrial-scale killing that ensued confounded the most seasoned commanders and terrorized the soldiers. As one American private would later write from the battlefront, "Ever since I volunteered I've felt like a cog in a huge wheel. The cog may get smashed up, but the machine goes on."

At first, Americans watched in horror from the sidelines. At the Battle of the Somme in 1916, 19,000 British soldiers died on the first day alone. American neutrality, meanwhile, was threatened at sea by the blockades mounted by German U-boats. In early 1917, Germany made the strategic gamble to commence unrestricted "sink on sight" submarine warfare to starve out the British, and President Wilson embraced American

▲ *Drafted recruits trade their civilian clothes for Army uniforms as they begin training at Camp Travis in San Antonio, Texas, c. 1917.*
National Archives

▶ *Scaling walls was part of the training for new soldiers at Camp Wadsworth, Spartanburg, South Carolina, c. 1918.*
Paul Thompson

entry into the war. "The world must be made safe for democracy," he vowed in his war message to Congress on April 2, 1917. Congress declared war four days later, and the Allies responded with an urgent demand for American troops.

But in 1917 the U.S. Army lacked the manpower and training to fight the war raging in Europe. Congress quickly passed the Selective Service Act in May 1917, requiring every man between the ages of 20 and 30 to register for military service. Local draft boards registered 24 million men, of whom 2.8 million were drafted, while another 2 million volunteered. Of the nearly 5 million men who served in the American armed forces (nearly one-fifth of them recent immigrants), 2 million served in France, half seeing combat.

▲ *A New York National Guardsman says goodbye to his sweetheart as his regiment leaves for Camp Wadsworth in South Carolina, c. 1917.*
National Archives

▶ *Standing at attention, women Marines prepare for a drill on the Ellipse, just south of the White House, in 1919.*
Library of Congress

American soldiers boarded ships for Europe with a great sense of mission, cheered on by patriotic parades. "We leave for 'over there' tonight, and I am thankful that I can take a place among men who will bring freedom to the world," wrote one private in July 1918. But "doughboys" arriving at the front were greeted by the hellish world of trench warfare, where rats and rotting corpses commingled. "Besides the desolation visible to the eye there was the desolation visible to the nose," one soldier wrote home in September 1917. The wet climate magnified the severity of trench life: "I stepped in a mud hole the other night and went up to my waist in mud and didn't get to change clothes and in fact I haven't changed yet," wrote one corporal in October 1918.

The defensive advantages of trenches were bolstered by the effective use of machine guns, snipers, field mines, and barbed-wire entanglements—all of which made the costs of infantry advances across "no man's land" unbearably high. Adding to the suffering was the novel use of tanks, aerial bombardment, and the first-ever use of chlorine and mustard gas. Over 70,000 American soldiers sustained poison-gas injuries, with nearly 1,500 killed. "If it hadn't been for the fellow with me I probably wouldn't be writing this letter," described one gas victim in 1917, "because I couldn't see, my eyes were running water and burning, so was my nose and I could hardly breathe." Another soldier dragged him a hundred yards to safety.

Yet the war's highest casualties came from artillery. Steel cannon firing high-explosive fragmentation shells reached their targets at a range of 20 miles. The high-pitched scream of an incoming shell offered the only warning of an imminent hit. Mortar shells, fired at a high angle over short distances, could hit trenches from close range. Mass production of armaments enabled a near-ceaseless barrage, and mounting head wounds from shrapnel led to the standard issue of the modern steel helmet, just as gas warfare led to the gas mask.

Three hundred eighty thousand African Americans served in the American forces during the war. With 200,000 sent to France, 42,000 were classified for combat but were completely segregated. In May 1918, the most famous African-American unit, the 369th Regiment, a group of volunteers from New York City, saw action with the French Army and earned the nickname "Harlem Hell Fighters" for their valor. The 369th was welcomed home with a triumphal parade down Fifth Avenue. After the war, the French government bestowed the Croix de Guerre on the entire regiment and awarded the Legion of Honor to 171 of its soldiers.

The call to duty also inspired 25,000 American women to volunteer. While many served in the Army or Navy Nurse Corps, others worked in France for the Red Cross and YMCA. American nurses tended the physical and emotional wounds of battered soldiers, while other women ran entertainment facilities, providing soldiers with much-needed escape from the horrors of the front. "If you want to do something for us," wrote a soldier to his family in North Carolina, "please boost the Y.M.C.A.—also the Red Cross. The Y.M.C.A. is our only home and the Red Cross girls our mother."

The first wave of the American Expeditionary Force (AEF) arrived in June 1917, but by the winter of 1917–1918 there were still fewer than 200,000 American soldiers in France. When the Germans launched a major offensive in March 1918, British and French commanders wanted American battalions deployed within their own regiments, but American commanders insisted on an independent force at the division level until a full American army could be established. It was not until July 1918—with over a million American soldiers in France—that American divisions fought alongside French divisions at the Second Battle of the Marne, ending the German offensive. This was followed in mid-September by the united American army fighting its first major battle, at St. Mihiel.

In late September, the Allies commenced the Meuse-Argonne offensive. In their biggest, fiercest operation of the war, 1.2 million American soldiers fought in densely wooded and hilly terrain; over 26,000 perished. Finally, Germany, exhausted and depleted, accepted an armistice on November 11, 1918—known to this day as Armistice Day in Europe and Veterans Day in America.

American soldiers eat lunch at their campsite mess tent in France, c. 1917.
Courtesy Corbis

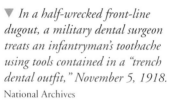 ▶ *A soldier writes home from the front-line trenches with his gun ready, December 17, 1917.*
Courtesy Corbis

▼ *In a half-wrecked front-line dugout, a military dental surgeon treats an infantryman's toothache using tools contained in a "trench dental outfit," November 5, 1918.*
National Archives

The war's grim effects, however, continued. Returning soldiers carried the Spanish flu back home. One of every five Americans was afflicted, and at least 500,000 died. An estimated 57,000 American soldiers succumbed to flu, as well—a toll higher than the U.S. army's combat deaths in France.

World War I brought the United States into Europe in an unprecedented way, setting the stage for future interventions there in World War II and during the Cold War. Except for the Interwar years of the 1920s and 1930s, American troops would garrison parts of Western Europe for the duration of the 20th century.

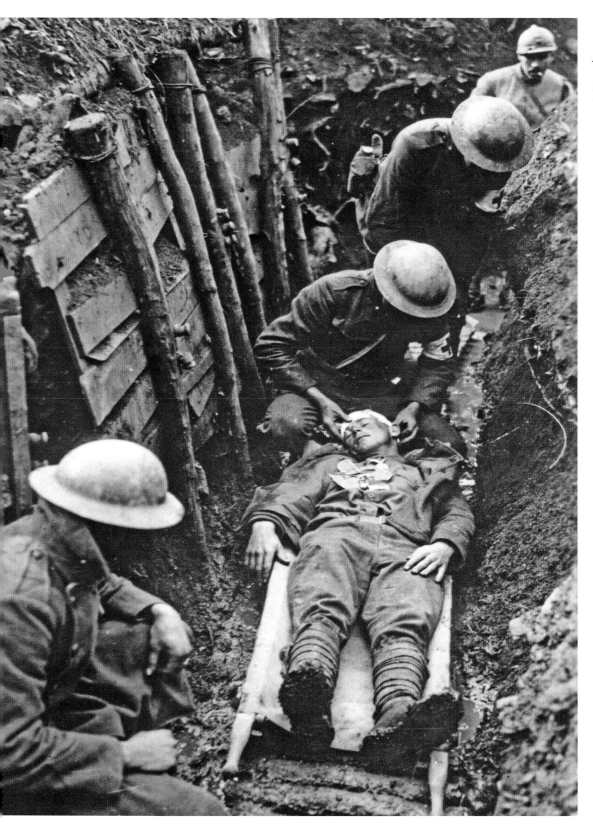

Wounded in the trenches near Verdun, France, a Marine receives first aid before being sent to a hospital, March 22, 1918.
Master Sgt. Leon H. Caverly/Signal Corps

▲ *An elderly French couple greets the American soldiers who ended a four-year German occupation of their village during an American advance on the Germans on November 6, 1918.*
Lt. Adrian C. Duff/Signal Corps

▶ *Americans enjoy captured German beer near Verdun, France, 1918.*
Courtesy Corbis

▲ *A wounded veteran watches a military parade of the 369th Colored Infantry,
also known as the "Harlem Hell Fighters," on February 17, 1919, in New York City.*
Courtesy Corbis

◀ *American troops march up Fifth Avenue in New York City in a homecoming
parade after the signing of the armistice that ended the war on November 11, 1918.*
National Archives

WORLD WAR II
1939 - 1945

I don't think any man can explain combat. It's beyond words. Take a combination of fear, anger, hunger, thirst, exhaustion, disgust, loneliness, homesickness, and wrap that all up in one reaction and you might approach the feelings a fellow has. It makes you feel mighty small, helpless, and alone.

> —Private Paul Curtis, writing from Anzio, Italy, May 28, 1944
> (Private Curtis was killed three days later, 15 miles from Rome.)

The largest and most violent conflict in human history, World War II enveloped the globe and mobilized belligerent societies in unprecedented ways. Referred to as the Good War by many Americans, the conflict pitted the Allied powers of the United States, the Soviet Union, and Great Britain against the Axis powers of Germany, Italy, and Japan, each of which had attacked its neighbors under the banner of imperial expansion. The threat posed to humanity by these aggressor states united Americans as no war before or since. From a nation of some 130 million people, 16 million American men and women served in uniform—four times the number mobilized in World War I.

The war began in Asia in July 1937 and in Europe in September 1939, but it was the entry of the United States in December 1941 that proved crucial to the Allied war effort. Collectively, the Allied powers ground down the war machines of the Axis tripartite, defeating Italy in September 1943, followed by Germany and Japan in May and August 1945, respectively.

American infantrymen wade ashore from Coast Guard landing craft at Normandy on D-Day, June 6, 1944.
Robert F. Sargent

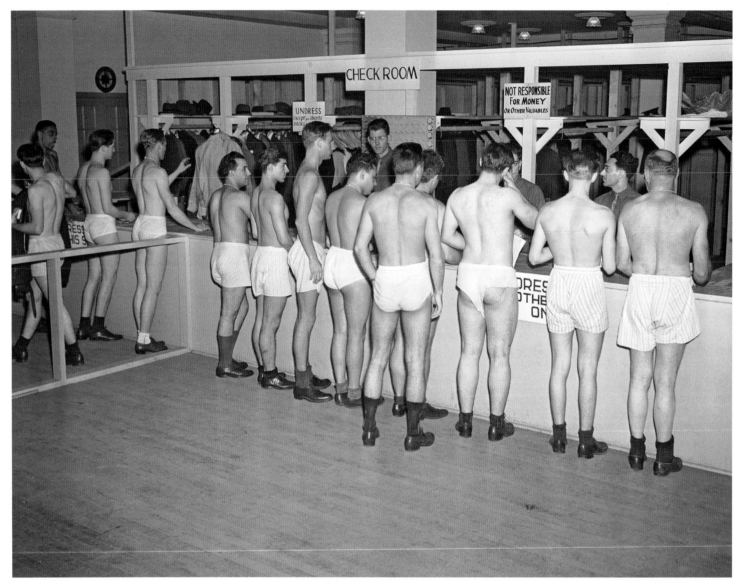

Enlistees prepare to undergo physical examinations at New York's Grand Central Palace, an induction center, in the fall of 1942.

Murray Becker/The Associated Press

The cost of victory was appalling. At least 60 million lives were lost worldwide—more than seven times the losses of World War I. While 95 percent of those killed in that earlier war were men in uniform, military deaths represented only 55 percent of the fatalities in World War II. Civilians had become acceptable targets for both sides, victims of the carpet bombing of dense urban centers and, above all, of the Holocaust orchestrated by Germany. With staggering military and civilian losses, the Soviet Union and China together bore well over half the entire death toll of the war, understandably so given that the extensive battlefronts in these two nations tied down roughly two-thirds of the German and Japanese ground forces, respectively. This factor ultimately saved the lives of American soldiers. Nonetheless, the United States not only raised the largest armed force in its history but also served as the chief arsenal and breadbasket of the Allied war effort—a stunning feat of national mobilization.

When the war began in Europe in the fall of 1939, the U.S. Army ranked eighteenth in size in the world, behind Romania and even small, neutral countries like Sweden and Portugal. But full mobilization and deployment brought the American soldier to battlefronts in almost every conceivable climate, from the frigid winters of Europe to the unbearable heat of the North African deserts and the tropical islands of the Pacific. The sons of World War I veterans were shipped off to parts of the globe that many of them,

Members of the U.S. Women's Army Corps in Southampton, England, board a troop transport bound for France, July 15, 1944.
Harcuardt/Signal Corps

before the war, could not have found on a map. "Well, I figure you're off on the Great Adventure," wrote one veteran of the American Expeditionary Force in WWI to his son, a private who would see combat in Europe. "You will see examples of selfishness and selflessness that will stir you tremendously. . . . I wish I could go FOR you, or at least WITH you, but this is your war."

Millions of former civilians had to be trained to destroy the enemy. "This week they are teaching us to kill," wrote one private from Minnesota. "I know how to break any hold or grip and throw a man flat on his face. They even teach us how to scientifically stomp on a man." But while the Army could train a soldier to kill, it could not suspend his natural emotions of fear and homesickness nor sustain morale amid horrific physical and mental conditions. Soldiers parachuted out of planes for the first time, spent days in foxholes under fire, and stormed fortified beaches not knowing whether they or their closest comrades would make it through alive. Along the battle lines they lived with few if any comforts, sleeping on the ground, enduring all weather conditions, and seldom being able to wash themselves. They lived off K rations, three-meal packets of bland food consisting of 3,000 calories and high in sugar and carbohydrates—a monotonous diet that at least quelled hunger and provided energy. Thirst, too, plagued men in battle, as reliable sources of safe water were often scarce.

The lives of countless American soldiers were saved, however, by advances in medicine and surgical techniques, and certainly by brave combat medics who offered emergency care and evacuation from the battlefield. Often armed with nothing more than Red Cross armbands and medical kits, they ran alongside infantry units, tending the wounded under fire. Bacterial infections, which in previous wars killed wounded men in droves, were abated dramatically by the discovery of antibiotic drugs such as penicillin and sulfanilamide. The impact of these medical gains was striking. Of all the American soldiers admitted to field hospitals and hospital ships in World War II, only 4 percent died, a mortality rate half that of World War I and miniscule compared to the estimated 50 percent of wounded men who died in the Civil War.

American women also joined the armed forces in record numbers. Across the various military branches, 350,000 served in uniform. Typically young single women, they came from all walks of life and for the first time served in many other capacities besides nursing. Through the military they discovered an opportunity to serve their country directly and to develop the kind of camaraderie with other women that their male counterparts had long valued among themselves in wartime. The Women's Army Corps (WACs) was the largest group in which women served—150,000 in all. When the WACs

American assault troops with full equipment move onto a beachhead in northern France on June 7, 1944, one day after D-Day.
Courtesy Corbis

were not deployed overseas, they performed many vital support functions stateside, allowing more men to deploy abroad. Another 75,000 women served in the Army and Navy Nurse Corps, many of them overseas in or near combat zones. In all, more than 400 military women lost their lives during World War II, 16 of them in action.

Soldiers fighting in the thick of war needed to take a break. Furloughs or passes for "rest and rehabilitation" (R&R) were issued for cities thought to be safe or for emergency leave home. Centers run by the USO (United Service Organizations) were established in major U.S. cities—for example, the Stage Door Canteen in New York—and close to training camps, and these clubs became soldiers' homes away from home. They offered chaperoned dances, reading rooms, big band performances, and a chance to spend time with carefully chosen young women. There were also traveling USO shows featuring Hollywood stars, like Bob Hope, who performed on makeshift stages close to the fighting front. And when, on August 25, 1944, American and British troops liberated Paris, the city soon became a favorite furlough destination for American soldiers. GIs fighting in the Pacific were given furloughs to Hawaii, which like Paris (and Nice, on the French Riviera) offered new social experiences for young American men who, before joining the army, had rarely been out of their home states.

Crossed rifles in the sand are a comrade's tribute to an American soldier who died at the barricades set up to block the Allied invasion force, 1944.
National Archives

German shells scream overhead as American infantrymen seek shelter alongside a tank. In the background are the ruins of Geich, a German town that fell to the Americans, December 11, 1944.
Signal Corps

In the European theater, American forces first landed in North Africa in November 1942, helping the British to push the German-Italian forces from the continent by May 1943. This was followed by the invasion of Sicily that July and mainland Italy in September. But the turning point for the Allies in Western Europe came with the Battle of Normandy in 1944, when they established their Western Front in France. Forty-seven Allied divisions gathered in England before the invasion: 21 American, 19 British, five Canadian, one French, and one Polish, for a total of 1.4 million troops. The most critical stage was D-Day, June 6, when the Allies first landed and secured a beachhead along a 50-mile stretch of extensively fortified shoreline. Unmatched in scale for an amphibious assault, the invasion—called Operation Overlord—moved a first wave of 175,000 soldiers and 30,000 vehicles across the English Channel in 12,000 planes and 6,000 warships, including 4,100 landing craft. For the American soldier in Europe, it was one of the most defining moments of the war. "With a stream of lead coming toward us," wrote one private of the D-Day landing, "we were at the mercy of the Germans. . . . Tried to land several places, but always had to withdraw. It was impossible to get ashore." His battalion was "almost wiped out," with 800 casualties out of 1,000 men.

But an Allied beachhead was secured, allowing the Allies to push on toward Germany. Progress was relatively smooth until December 16, when the Germans launched their last-ditch offensive, along the German-Belgian border. Amid the coldest and snowiest weather in memory, the so-called Battle of the Bulge caught the Allies by surprise. Engaging 600,000 American troops, the 40-day battle was the largest ever fought by the U.S. army. It was also the bloodiest engagement for American forces in all of World War II, with 83,000 American casualties, of whom 19,000 were killed and 23,500 captured. The German gamble failed, however, and the Anglo-American forces resumed their offensive into Germany from the west while Soviet forces closed in on Berlin from the east. On May 8, 1945, the Germans surrendered. (The date became known as V-E Day, for Victory in Europe.)

◀ *After his first night of combat during the Battle of the Bulge, Cpl. Frank Johnson of Brooklyn was sent to a depot to get blankets and ammo for his unit, December 1944.*
National Archives

▲ *Americans of the 347th Infantry are
served chow on the frigid road to La
Roche, Belgium, January 13, 1945.*
Signal Corps

▲ *American soldiers captured by the Germans in the Battle of the Bulge line up for a march to a POW camp, January 18, 1945.*
Courtesy The Associated Press

◄ *A German officer who was hiding in a building in Illy, France, is captured by an American infantryman in September 1944.*
Courtesy The Associated Press

▶ *Soldiers of the 9th Infantry, under heavy German attack, dash across a pontoon bridge over the Rur River in the Rhineland. The body of an American soldier lies sprawled before them.*
George Silk/Time Life Pictures/Getty Images

A Frenchwoman exclaims to neighbors and an American soldier, "All Belfort is liberated," November 25, 1944.
Leibowitz/Signal Corps

Liberated prisoners in the Mauthausen concentration camp near Linz, Austria, cheer the cavalrymen of the 11th Armored Division. The banner across the wall was made by Spanish Loyalist prisoners, May 6, 1945.
Pfc. Donald R. Ornitz/Signal Corps

▲ 1st Sgt. Rance Richardson, a veteran of two wars, takes a break during fighting on Bougainville in the South Pacific, April 4, 1944.
Shuman/Signal Corps

◄ U.S. soldiers, bearded and weary, plod along a road toward an American base of operations in Guadalcanal, Solomon Islands, after 21 days of fighting the Japanese, February 1943.
Courtesy The Associated Press

The early months of U.S. engagement in the Pacific theater were marked by setbacks. The biggest occurred on April 9, 1942, when the Japanese forced the surrender of 75,000 American and Philippine soldiers on the Bataan Peninsula, across the bay from Manila on the Philippine island of Luzon. It was the largest surrender of U.S. forces in history. The Japanese then forced their captives, already emaciated by hunger, to march 90 miles to a prisoner-of-war camp—a trek known as the Bataan Death March. Only 54,000 men reached the camp. A number managed to escape en route, but somewhere between 6,000 and 11,000 men died along the way; some were executed by their captors. The defeat of the last U.S. forces in the archipelago, on the island of Corregidor on May 6, marked the fall of the Philippines. A U.S. territory secured in war was now lost in war.

Shortly thereafter, however, the tide turned. With the Battle of Midway in June 1942, followed by the Battle of Guadalcanal, which lasted from August 1942 through February 1943, the Japanese offensive was halted. It was at Guadalcanal, in the southern Solomon Islands, that American soldiers secured the first defeat of Japanese ground forces.

▲ *A Marine, his face grimy with coral dust, carries the fatigue of battle after two days and nights of hell on the beach of Eniwetok in the Marshall Islands, February 1944.*

National Archives

▶ *American troops, under cover of palm trees, hit the beach at Rendova Island in the Solomons, June 1943.*

National Archives

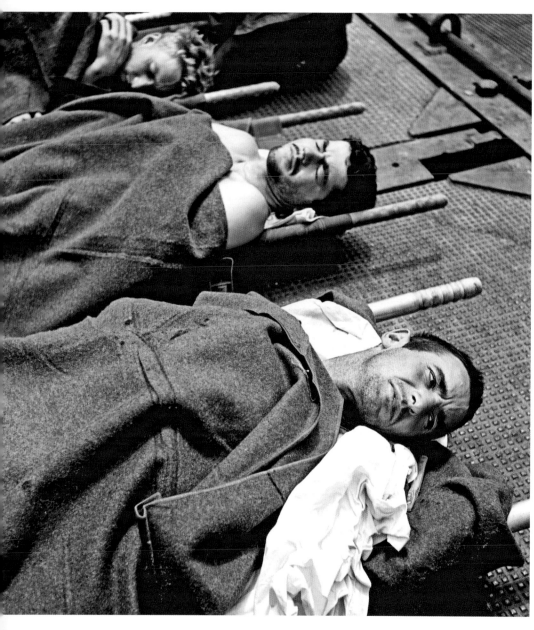

▲ GIs wounded on Okinawa wait for transportation to a hospital ship anchored off the shore of Okinawa, May 1945.

Courtesy Corbis

▶ In an underground surgery room, an Army doctor operates on a GI wounded by a Japanese sniper on Bougainville in the Solomon Islands, December 12, 1943.

Signal Corps

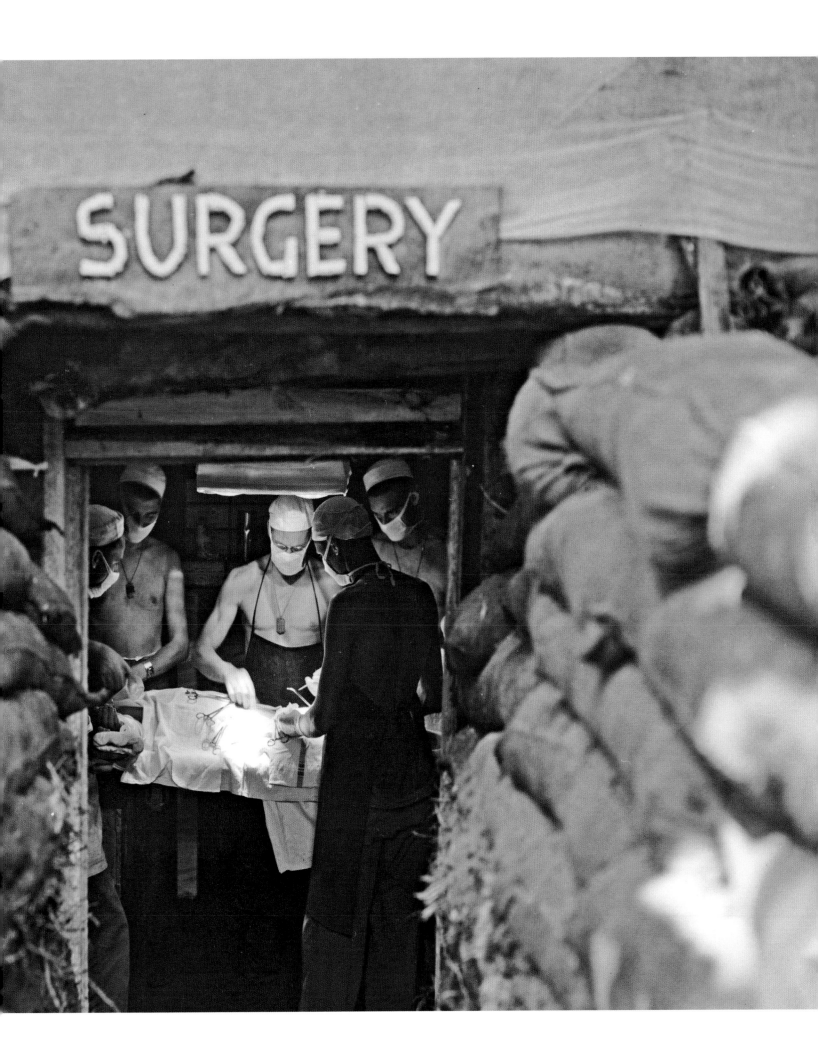

Navajo Indian code talkers landed with the first Marine assault on Saipan, transmitting radio and telephone messages in their native language—a code the Japanese were unable to break. Philippines, June 1944.

J. L. Burns/ Marine Corps

▲ *The Bataan Death March, from Bataan to the prison camp at Cabanatuan in the Philippines, traversed 90 miles in six days. American prisoners, hands tied, marched without food and water.*

Marine Corps

▶ *This captured Japanese photograph shows American soldiers and sailors who surrendered to Japanese forces on Corregidor in the Philippines, May 1942.*

Signal Corps

The American strategy in the Pacific called for an "island hopping" campaign in which islands heavily fortified by the Japanese were bypassed in favor of invading less strongly defended ones. This strategy clearly saved American lives as U.S. forces pushed northward from Australia and westward from Hawaii in 1942 and 1943. By October 1944, American forces returned to the Philippines, followed in early 1945 by the critical invasions of Iwo Jima in February and Okinawa in April. In both battles, American soldiers faced incredible resistance from Japanese forces bunkered in camouflaged caves, tunnels, and pillboxes. Okinawa was the bloodiest battle in the Pacific theater. For 82 days, 180,000 American troops battled 100,000 Japanese soldiers who fought to the bitter end in what was the final major battle of the war. Securing the island came at an enormous cost in American lives, with 51,000 casualties, among them 12,500 killed. In fact, nearly half the American fatalities in the Pacific occurred in the battles of Okinawa and Iwo Jima.

Pfc. Rez Hester, 7th War Dog Platoon, naps while Butch, his war dog, stands guard, Iwo Jima, 1945. Fifteen platoons of War Dogs started training in 1942.
Sgt. S. Kaufman/ Marine Corps

From their base of operations in Okinawa, just 350 miles from the major islands of the Japanese chain, American commanders planned the invasion of Japan. Slated for November 1945, Operation Downfall, involving 5 million American troops, would have dwarfed D-Day. In August, however, the dropping of atomic bombs on Hiroshima and Nagasaki, as well as the Soviet Union's declaration of war against Japan, secured the Japanese surrender. On V-J Day, as on V-E Day, servicemen and civilians alike crowded streets around the world to celebrate peace with great fanfare.

The "Good War" was a necessary war, and American soldiers could take comfort that their sacrifices helped free millions of people from brutal occupations. Civilians from

An American soldier rescues a Japanese baby found at "Death Valley" in the hills of Saipan Island in Micronesia, where hundreds of Japanese soldiers and their families committed suicide rather than surrender, July 20, 1944.
Courtesy Corbis

France to the Philippines greeted U.S. forces with deep gratitude. But nothing could prepare the victorious troops for the horrors they would witness at the concentration camps. "In two years of combat you can imagine I have seen a lot of death, furious deaths mostly," wrote one sergeant home after liberating the camp at Dachau. "But nothing has ever stirred me as much as this. . . . How can people do things like that? I never believed they could until now." An American POW, liberated from a camp inside Germany, wrote of the arrival of U.S. troops: "It was indeed a spectacle that I'll never be able to fully describe—to be one of 175,000 prisoners in this camp and see them all, English, Poles, Indians, Russians, Senegalese, French, and Americans, fall to their knees to pray as they watched the American Flag rise over this 'hellhole.'"

Victory for America came at the expense of 405,000 dead (292,000 in battle) and 670,000 wounded. Another 125,000 were prisoners of war. In the end, the European theater had proved far more costly than the Pacific, accounting for nine-tenths of America's fatalities and four-fifths of its wounded. In fact, the 41,000 American lives lost defeating Japan amounted to a smaller toll than America would suffer in either Korea or Vietnam. Although President Harry S. Truman wanted to maintain a postwar army of 1.5 million, Congress and the American public did not. By 1947 the army stood at 700,000—only the sixth largest among the world's armies. But the further deterioration of Soviet-American relations that year would lead to the Cold War and stir the national appetite for rearmament—and with it a new set of wars for the American soldier to fight.

American servicemen and women celebrate in the streets of Paris on V-J Day, the day Japan surrendered, ending World War II, August 14, 1945.
Stars and Stripes

KOREAN WAR
1950 - 1953

No matter what you read, or are told, it's no fun dodging bullets and artillery shells, never knowing from day to day whether you'll ever see your home, family or parents again—no, it's a Hell on earth.

> —Pfc. Jack Train, Jr., writing from Korea, May 29, 1953
>
> (Private Train was killed on July 7, 1953, 21 days before a cease-fire was declared.)

The Korean War, often referred to as the "Forgotten War," appears lost to American public memory between the heroism of World War II and the controversies of Vietnam. But for the 5.7 million American men and women who served in the armed services during the conflict it was far from forgettable. Just five years after V-J Day marked the end of the Allied war against imperial Japan, the United States was again embroiled in a major war in East Asia, this time on the Korean peninsula, fighting the Communist powers in the region.

The Korean War lasted five months longer and cost more American lives than did America's participation in the Pacific theater of World War II. Of the 1.5 million Americans deployed in Korea, 36,500 were killed (33,700 in battle), while another 103,000 were wounded. Of the 7,000 American prisoners of war, an alarming two out of five did not survive confinement. Not only was Korea the first crisis of the Cold War to escalate into a full military conflict, but it was also the first major war waged without a formal declaration of war from Congress, treated instead as a United Nations "police action" by the president.

A gunner, with assistance from his gun crew, fires a 75mm recoilless rifle near Oetlook-tong, Korea, June 9, 1951.
Peterson/U.S. Army

The rugged and mountainous terrain of Korea proved treacherous for the American soldier, as its winding hills and narrow valleys afforded the enemy opportunities for surprise attack and escape. "If the best minds in the world had set out to find us the worst possible location to fight a war," declared Secretary of State Dean Acheson, "the unanimous choice would have to be Korea."

Korea's brutal, windswept winters forced soldiers to endure some of the worst battle conditions ever faced by American forces. At the Battle of the Chosin Reservoir in late November and early December 1950, temperatures plummeted to 30 degrees below zero, resulting in 7,500 frostbite casualties among the roughly 30,000 American-led UN troops. Surrounded by 120,000 enemy troops, they had to fight their way out, at the cost of 2,500 killed and another 5,000 wounded. "I have never seen anything like what I just went thru," wrote one private, recovering from frostbite, to his father. "The 'Vets' of World War II agree also, that this is the worst they have seen." Of the 180 men in his battery, only 42 remained alive—and 32 of those survivors were wounded.

The Korean War marked the first time American soldiers fought in desegregated units. After President Harry S. Truman ended racial discrimination in the armed forces in 1948, African-American troops were no longer required to fight separately, live in separate barracks, or dine in separate mess halls. Moving beyond the traditional support units, they served in combat roles and fought in every major operation in Korea. When the war began, the nearly 100,000 African Americans in the U.S. military constituted about 8 percent of total forces. By war's end, an estimated 600,000 would serve.

The Women's Armed Services Act of 1948 opened the military as a career for women in peacetime, but their numbers as a percentage of overall personnel declined from World War II. During the years of the Korean War, 120,000 served in the armed forces, up from the 22,000 on active duty when the war broke out. Many of them, especially nurses, were veterans of World War II. And many nurses served in or near combat zones. Several even came ashore with the Marines at Inchon. Amid battle conditions, nurses donned helmets, fatigues, and combat boots, much like the men they tended. Off the battlefield, there were pressing needs for women in support roles. Each branch had its female corps, the largest being the Women's Army Corps (the WACs), which recruited volunteers as well as recalling women (including married women) to active duty. Korea marked the first war in which women were called to active duty beyond their voluntary tours.

Critical to the treatment of wounded soldiers was the Mobile Army Surgical Hospital, or MASH unit. These new units brought the personnel and expertise of a full hospital much closer to the front lines. The wounded, after being treated on the battlefield and stabilized at an aid station, were then transferred to the MASH units. Critical surgical care near the battle lines, in addition to the first-time use of helicopters to evacuate the wounded to MASH units, saved the lives of many soldiers. Among patients treated at MASH units in Korea, the fatality rate was only 3 percent.

U.S. Marines pose for a group picture soon after
North Korean forces swept across the 38th
parallel and invaded South Korea, 1950.
Courtesy David Douglas Duncan Photography
Collection, Harry Ransom Humanities Research Center,
University of Texas at Austin

But the combat helicopter, which saw its first wide-scale use in the Korean War, did much more than transport the wounded. The new aircraft vastly expanded the tactical mobility of U.S. ground forces. Initially used to scout forward terrain and enemy positions, in time helicopters helped resupply, redeploy, and rescue frontline troops. And just as the helicopter proved indispensable to American soldiers' efforts on the ground, so, too, did the jet aircraft. For the first time, jets provided air support to American troops. Even so, air power alone could not determine the outcome of the war. That burden, as in World War II, fell on the ground forces.

In Korea, the American soldier fought for what had long been a coveted piece of real estate—a peninsula (about the size of Kansas) encircled by China, Russia, and Japan. All three had fought imperial wars over its control until a victorious Japan made Korea a colony in 1905. Following the defeat of Japan in World War II, the United States and the Soviet Union created postwar occupation zones using the 38th parallel as a demarcation line, a spot determined by two U.S. colonels using nothing more than a National Geographic Society map. But after Soviet and American forces left the peninsula in 1949, tensions escalated between the rival Democratic People's Republic of Korea in the North and the Republic of Korea in the South. The problem was magnified by the larger tensions of the Cold War in East Asia. In 1949, the Soviet Union detonated its first atomic bomb, ending the American nuclear monopoly, while the Communists won control of mainland China. There they established the People's Republic of China, while the American-backed Nationalist forces evacuated to the island of Formosa (Taiwan), where they declared the Republic of China. As had already happened in Europe, Asia was being rapidly divided along Cold War lines.

Then, with Soviet consent and military aid, North Korea broke the impasse, launching a full-scale invasion of South Korea in the predawn hours of June 25, 1950. The surprise attack stunned the United States and its allies in the United Nations. That very day the Security Council convened an emergency session, passing two unprecedented resolutions by unanimous vote: the first demanding that North Korea withdraw from South Korea, the second granting the use of force by UN member nations to enforce the first resolution. Ordinarily, the Soviet Union would have vetoed such resolutions, but it was then boycotting the UN for its refusal to admit the People's Republic of China.

Having mobilized American and UN support for armed intervention in Korea, President Truman sought to limit the hostilities to Korea. Many feared the crisis could escalate into a general war in East Asia involving Soviet and Chinese troops. Such a scenario might trigger a Soviet counterstrike in Europe. In short, Truman did not want Korea to spark World War III, especially when both sides now had atomic bombs. This difficult task required maintaining solid UN and NATO support while rearming the American and allied forces to wage a "limited war" in Korea. Sixteen UN member states joined U.S. forces in Korea, although South Korea and the United States each provided nearly half of the coalition's land forces, and the United States supplied roughly 90 percent of its naval and air strength.

In early July 1950, U.S. ground forces that had been stationed in Occupied Japan landed at the strategic port of Pusan in southeastern Korea to aid the beleaguered South Korean forces while waiting for reinforcements to arrive in strength. But the Americans sustained heavy losses and by early August were driven back to the Pusan perimeter, an area covering just 10 percent of the peninsula. To break the tide of the North Korean

Marines clamber up scaling ladders to storm ashore at Inchon in an amphibious invasion, September 15, 1950.
Staff Sgt. W.W. Frank/U.S. Marines

offensive, the UN coalition on September 15 made a daring landing well behind enemy lines at the port of Inchon in northwestern South Korea. This stunning amphibious invasion forced the North Korean forces into a hasty retreat toward the 38th parallel by month's end. The liberation of South Korea was achieved in less than three months.

But the liberation offered the United States and its UN allies a fateful choice: either reinforce the prewar border and initiate peace negotiations or pursue the North Koreans across the 38th parallel and reunify Korea. Opinion polls showed that a majority of Americans, as well as a number of UN allies, backed armed reunification. On October 7, 1950, the UN General Assembly passed a resolution to "reunify and rehabilitate" Korea, allowing UN forces to cross the 38th parallel to do so.

◀ *Korean winters were so frigid that GIs such as this hooded fighter had trouble breaking loose a single frost-coated bean from a can, December 1950.*

Courtesy David Douglas Duncan Photography Collection, Harry Ransom Humanities Research Center, University of Texas at Austin

▶ *Marines charge toward the enemy's position, taking little note of a dead enemy soldier as they advance, September 1950.*

Courtesy David Douglas Duncan Photography Collection, Harry Ransom Humanities Research Center, University of Texas at Austin

American and South Korean forces crossed the 38th parallel on October 9. But the action provoked China, which secretly sent "volunteers" across the Yalu River to support North Korea. When South Korean forces reached the Yalu on October 25, Chinese troops smashed their lines and then pulled back, arguably as a warning to the UN coalition. But American commanders pressed the UN forces northward, even launching a "final" offensive on November 24. The next day, however, 270,000 Chinese troops formally joined North Korean forces in a surprise counterattack that threw the UN forces into a southward retreat. By late December, Soviet MiG-15 jets (some with Soviet pilots) were providing air cover up to 60 miles north of the battlefront. America's "limited war" in Korea had widened.

By January 1951, with Chinese and North Korean forces advancing below the 38th parallel, the United States and its UN allies decided on a new aim: stabilize the front and pursue a negotiated settlement. Yet both sides launched massive offensives and counteroffensives that over the next six months saw the battle lines ebb and flow across the 38th parallel. The "police action" had clearly become a full-scale war, and the inconclusive fighting took its toll on troop morale. "I sure hope that it will all be over soon," wrote one

A grief-stricken American infantryman whose buddy was killed in action is comforted by another GI as a medic methodically fills out the casualty tags, Haktong-ni, Korea, August 28, 1950.

Sgt. Al Chang/Signal Corps

sergeant to his wife in February. "I am sick of this whole mess over here." By July 1951, deep in a stalemate of trench warfare, both sides called for armistice negotiations.

The talks dragged on for two years while the brutal fighting continued, with enormous costs for soldiers and civilians alike. For many American soldiers, the plight of Korean civilians caught in the battle lines was particularly difficult to witness. "I feel terribly sorry for the refugees," wrote one private. "They seem so miserable and all are hungry and cold. We're letting them sit by the fire and are feeding them." The war created more than a million Korean refugees, including thousands of orphans. "Even if the war did end," wrote one sergeant to his wife, "there is no place for anybody to go. No homes, no food, and for thousands of kids, there are no parents. I wish I could bring one of them home with me. . . . I found one yesterday in a house, sitting on the floor crying her little heart out. Everybody else was dead."

Pfc. Clarence Whitmore, voice radio operator, 24th Infantry Regiment, reads the latest news in Stars and Stripes *during a lull in battle, near Sangju, Korea, August 9, 1950.*
Pfc. Charles Fabiszak/Army

▲ *Pfc. Edward Wilson of the 24th Infantry Regiment, wounded in action, awaits evacuation to an aid station behind the lines, February 16, 1951.*
Pfc. Charles Fabiszak/Signal Corps

▶ *A machine gun crew rests after an assault on a Chinese position. Frigid winters and sweltering summer heat hampered American advances.*
Courtesy Bevin Alexander

Half of all the American deaths in the war occurred after the armistice talks began. And the costs of the four-year war were enormous for a country as small as Korea. An estimated 2 million Koreans died, more than three-quarters of them civilians. Millions of others were displaced.

Not until July 1953 was a cease-fire secured. Even then, no official peace treaty was ever signed, and more than half a century later 37,000 American soldiers remain in South Korea to preserve the armistice. Moreover, the Korean War led to the permanent rearmament of the American military; its budget more than quadrupled during the war, never to return to prewar levels. Many more American men would find themselves as career soldiers. Nor was Korea the last war they would fight to contain communism in Asia.

VIETNAM WAR
1965 - 1973

Last night one more Marine died. No one will ever hear or care about it except his parents and us. There is no nation to mourn for him or fly our flag at half mast. Yet this Marine did more for his country than any President or Senator ever did. . . . He was a good Marine and a better person. He didn't deserve dying in a damn country not worth fightin' for. But he is dead and those back home whose freedom he was defending will never know his name.

> —L. Cpl. Stephen Daniel, Marines, writing
> from Vietnam, August 9, 1968

No war except the Civil War divided the American people more deeply than Vietnam. Nor did any American war last longer. Although the official engagement of U.S. combat forces in Vietnam lasted from 1965 to 1973 (eight years to the month), American involvement in Vietnam actually spanned a quarter-century, under six consecutive U.S. presidents. From the aid that the United States funneled into the French-Indochinese War in 1950 through the fall of Saigon in 1975, Vietnam was the greatest flashpoint of U.S. foreign policy in the Cold War era. During the combat stage of the U.S. war in Vietnam, 8.7 million men and women served in the U.S. armed forces worldwide, and two out of five of them were deployed in Southeast Asia. Among the 3.4 million U.S. troops sent to fight that war, 58,000 were killed (47,000 in battle) and another 153,000 wounded (75,000 severely disabled)—casualties that, across the board, were higher than those America sustained in the Pacific theater of World War II.

U.S. artillerymen, forced to abandon Firebase Annie under North Vietnamese pressure, head for a helicopter at Bu Prang Special Forces camp near the Cambodian border, November 3, 1969.
Horst Faas/The Associated Press

No one doubts that the American soldier paid the highest price for the country's controversial war in Vietnam. Yet how the world's most powerful nation failed to quell a guerilla insurgency in a peasant society remains a topic of continued debate.

The American war in Southeast Asia had its origins in the French-Indochinese War (1946–1954), which began when France tried to reassert its colonial claims over Indochina (Vietnam, Laos, and Cambodia) following World War II. Despite enormous U.S. aid, the French were defeated by the Vietnamese communists at Dien Bien Phu in 1954. That same year, the Geneva Accords ended French rule in Indochina and temporarily divided Vietnam at the 17th parallel between a communist North and a noncommunist South, with a national election set for 1956. That this election was never held contributed to the second

◄ *Soldiers of the U.S. Army 11th Armored Cavalry Regiment arrive in Vung Tau, South Vietnam, in 1966.*
Henri Huet/The Associated Press

▲ *A Marine, camouflaged and armed, is ready for a reconnaissance patrol in Vietnam, April 1967.*
National Archives

Vietnamese war, which lasted from 1959 to 1975. Just as the insurgency of the southern communists, known as the Viet Cong, depended on support from the Democratic Republic of Vietnam in the North, the survival of the Republic of Vietnam in the South depended on U.S. assistance. But despite ever-increasing amounts of aid and the thousands of U.S. military "advisers" sent to South Vietnam, the American-backed regime in South Vietnam was on the verge of collapse by 1963–1964. In March 1965, President Lyndon B. Johnson made the fateful decision to deploy U.S. ground forces in South Vietnam and to commence a bombing campaign against North Vietnam—thus the "Americanization" of the war.

Vietnam offered geographic obstacles far worse than those faced by American soldiers in Korea. Although the total landmass of North and South Vietnam together was only a little larger than New Mexico, the narrow, divided country stretched for more than a thousand miles from north to south—roughly the distance from Los Angeles to Seattle. Vietnam's extensive coastline meandered for some 2,000 miles—a length greater than the U.S. border with Mexico. And South Vietnam's porous interior border with Cambodia and Laos was 800 miles long, or about the length of the California coast. For U.S. forces to control these borders and prevent the North Vietnamese from supplying the Viet Cong in the South proved virtually impossible. Nor could U.S. forces effectively prevent North Vietnam from receiving aid from China and the Soviet Union without risking an expanded war.

Marines are silhouetted at an airstrip at Dong Ha, eight miles south of the demilitarized zone between North and South Vietnam, as they make their way to an assault against the North Vietnamese, July 19, 1966.
Horst Faas/The Associated Press

Vietnam's rainforests, which even the massive amounts of chemical defoliants sprayed on them could not denude, also proved difficult for the American soldier. The jungle offered the enemy cover for ambushes on U.S. troops. Although the Americans possessed the ostensible advantages of air support and powerful artillery, these proved nearly useless when Viet Cong units hit American units at close range. "It will never cease to amaze me how unorthodox this war seems compared to how I imagined it," wrote one private in 1969. "There are no set lines of battle & it is usually over as fast as it starts." Guerilla attacks, coupled with land mines and booby traps, made "search and destroy" missions nightmarish tasks for American soldiers, exacting heavy losses and draining their morale.

Identifying the enemy among the local population posed another dilemma for the American soldier. Patrolling any village suspected of supporting the Viet Cong was fraught with peril. "Everyone is nervous when moving in," wrote one soldier home in 1970. "All it takes is one person firing in the air, and everyone assumes that there is contact and they are under fire. . . .Then, with everyone firing in all directions, people get carried away, like a mob. Everyone is doing it, but no one is leading it." American soldiers often found the situation difficult to describe, or justify, to those back home. "They've never had a friend hit a booby trap and shipped the pieces home in a rubber sack," agonized the same soldier.

Marines take cover at a stone gate of the Citadel, one of the ancient capital of Hue's landmark structures.
Kyoichi Sawada/UPI

Paratroopers of the U.S. 2nd Battalion, 173rd Airborne Brigade, cross a river in the rain during a search for Viet Cong in the jungle area of Ben Cat, South Vietnam, September 25, 1965.

Henri Huet/The Associated Press

Vietnam was the first "televised" war, and the medium transformed how Americans got their war coverage. During World War II and the Korean War, news organizations had typically offered carefully edited newsreels and radio reports, but now graphic, uncensored images were broadcast daily into American homes. Whether televised reports actually shaped or followed the public's mood about the war is widely debated, but the "up close and personal style" of field reports nonetheless conveyed the chaos of battle and the agony of loss in the actual faces and voices of American soldiers.

Securing enough soldiers to fight the war was a troublesome problem. In the mid-1960s, the rapidly increasing demand for more troops led to rising draft calls, from 100,000 in 1964 up to 400,000 in 1966. Nearly 27 million men reached draft age between 1964 and 1973, yet 16 million of them did not serve in the military, and all but 4 percent of these received legal deferments and exemptions. The deferments granted university students shifted the burden of the draft onto the working class and poor. Meanwhile, exemptions for conscientious objectors—which accounted for only 0.15 percent of exemptions in World War II and 1.5 percent in Korea—reached 8 percent in 1967 and a staggering 43 percent by 1971. A quarter-million eligible men never registered at all, while about half a million defied draft calls. Upwards of 50,000 went into exile; thousands burned their draft cards in protest. In 1969, efforts were made to reform the Selective Service system, including an annual draft lottery that ended most deferments, but the draft itself became another casualty of the war when the All-Volunteer Armed Force (AVF) was established in 1973.

▲ *Wounded Marines rest in the red mud of a first aid center as they await helicopter evacuation to a hospital. This fighting took place near the demilitarized zone in 1966.*
Larry Burrows

▶ *Soldiers of the 1st U.S. Air Cavalry carry their dead comrade through the jungle. He was killed by a sniper after the futile search through a village for Viet Cong, September 16, 1966.*
Courtesy The Associated Press

Wounded medic Thomas Cole of Richmond, Virginia,
continues to treat Staff Sgt. Harrison Pell during a firefight
in the South Vietnamese highlands, January 30, 1966.
Henri Huet/The Associated Press

The proportion of African Americans serving in the Vietnam War was the highest in any American war up to that time. African Americans made up 11 percent of the national population at the height of the Vietnam War in 1965–1969, yet they accounted for 12.6 percent of the soldiers deployed in Vietnam, a majority of them in the army infantry. Even though the total percentage of African-American fatalities was roughly proportionate to their deployment, they suffered nearly 15 percent of all combat deaths from 1965 to 1969. As the number of blacks in the military grew, issues of racial justice came to the fore: by 1968, racial violence on military bases led to interracial councils and sensitivity training. Military commanders found these novel initiatives critical in maintaining troop morale and fighting strength.

A Marine pauses as his combat patrol crosses a jungle stream south of Khe Sanh, South Vietnam, in an effort to find and destroy enemy arms caches, March 29, 1969.
Courtesy The Associated Press

Two Vietnamese children gaze at a U.S. paratrooper holding an M79 grenade launcher as they huddle against a canal bank for protection from Viet Cong sniper fire, January 1, 1966.

Horst Faas/The Associated Press

A Vietnamese villager clutches her hat and an American soldier leans a weary head on his hand as they sit together after a battle with the Viet Cong, 290 miles from Saigon, February 5, 1966.

Rick Merron/The Associated Press

The changing role of women in the 1960s also influenced the military during the Vietnam War. Although the 1948 Women's Armed Services Act had opened a permanent role for women in the armed forces, the act had capped female enlistment at 2 percent of active-duty personnel and prohibited women from being promoted above the rank of lieutenant colonel. In 1967, however, recruiting deficits forced the removal of these restrictions. Nearly 7,500 women served in Vietnam, over four-fifths of them as branch military nurses, eight of whom died. In the aftermath of the war, the number of women grew dramatically, from 1.6 percent of active-duty personnel in 1971 to 5 percent by 1976.

But these reforms did not lead to success in Vietnam. Having assumed responsibility for fighting the war in South Vietnam in 1965, the United States failed to achieve political stability by military means, which led to the steady escalation of U.S. troops

there, from 185,000 at the end of 1965 to more than 500,000 in 1968. That January, however, the North Vietnamese Army and the Viet Cong launched the Tet Offensive, a gamble aimed at breaking the stalemate through a massive countrywide attack against U.S. and South Vietnamese positions. Although the brutal campaign ended as a tactical military defeat for the communist forces, it afforded them a strategic psychological victory. It exposed the failures of U.S. counterinsurgency efforts and belied ongoing claims of progress made to the American public. The political fallout was tremendous. In March, President Johnson agreed to halt the bombing of North Vietnam, rejected a call for 200,000 more troops, and offered to engage in peace negotiations with Hanoi. In a stunning move, he also declined to seek reelection that year. With a policy of disengagement decided upon, the Paris peace talks began in May 1968.

The opposition to the war by a majority of the American public after Tet stemmed from the war's escalating costs in American lives and taxes and from growing doubts about whether the war could be won at a reasonable cost—or won at all. American soldiers, who were still being sent to Vietnam in droves, voiced their frustration: "One thing is very evident since having more contact with returning troops & that is that no one really feels like he is a great patriot or that he has fought for any apparent justifiable reason," wrote one private to his parents from basic training in 1969. "Going to Nam, for the soldier, is simply an unavoidable obligation that one has to fight to stay alive to finish."

Expecting that incoming President Richard M. Nixon could achieve his campaign pledge of "peace with honor," many Americans in 1969 could not have imagined that U.S. combat forces would remain in Vietnam for another four years, with the additional loss of more than 20,000 American lives. Indeed, U.S. efforts toward the "Vietnamization" of the war were conflicting. The steady withdrawal of U.S. forces began in June 1969 and continued apace, with little more than 150,000 troops left by the end of 1971. But to force concessions from North Vietnam at the peace table, President Nixon resumed the bombing campaign against the North. To root out camps and destroy supply lines in Cambodia and Laos, he also ordered U.S. and South Vietnamese forces to invade those countries in April 1970 and February 1971, respectively. In effect, Nixon had expanded the war.

After nearly four years of political negotiations that went on as the fighting continued, the Paris Peace Accords were signed on January 27, 1973. When the last American combat troops left Vietnam on March 29, America's longest and most divisive war came to an unceremonious end. After a quarter-century of American efforts to prevent a unified communist Vietnam, the fall of Saigon to the North Vietnamese in April 1975 accomplished both. Some consider the Vietnam War to be not only the greatest tragedy in the history of U.S. foreign relations but also the most futile war the American soldier was ever ordered to fight. Others, however, continue to view the war as having been vital to holding the global "containment" line against communism, and they credit America's failure to do so in South Vietnam to a lack of political will. Regardless of the interpretation, the Vietnam War was a brutal time for American soldiers, many of whom still suffer the traumas of their Vietnam experience.

A Vietnam veteran holds his baby
while watching a Veterans Day parade
in Chattanooga, Tennessee, in 1976.
Courtesy of Robin Hood, 1977 Pulitzer Prize

GULF WAR
1990 - 1991

It never seemed like a war. More like a field problem. Even when stuff was burning all around you and firing going off all over the place. It was very real, but more a curiosity than anything else. . . . This [ground war] only lasted four days. It wasn't even long enough to seem like a war.

—S. Sgt. Dan Welch, First Infantry Division, writing from Saudi Arabia, March 8, 1991

During the Cold War, U.S. military concerns had concentrated largely on Western Europe and East Asia, but the focal point abruptly shifted to the Middle East just as the Soviet-American rivalry was winding down. On August 2, 1990, just nine months after the fall of the Berlin Wall, Iraqi forces invaded Kuwait— placing one-fifth of the world's known oil reserves under Iraqi dictator Saddam Hussein's control. With Saddam's armed forces poised inside Kuwait just north of Saudi Arabia's primary oil fields, an Iraqi advance just a few hundred miles southward would give Saddam custody of one-third of the world's reserves.

The strategic implications were profound. Iraq, a nation roughly the size of California and with only 19 million people, had amassed the world's fourth-largest standing army, with 900,000 soldiers. Saddam believed that the Arab states would tolerate his territorial grab, and he thought that the United States and its allies would shy away from military intervention. To some extent, Saddam based his belief on U.S. behavior in Vietnam and during the Iranian Hostage Crisis (1979–1981), convincing himself that America had little appetite for high casualties or the threat of a protracted war. These were grave miscalculations.

After the departure of U.S. combat forces from Vietnam in 1973, U.S. military actions, including those in Grenada in October 1983 and Panama in December 1989, had been brief and minor in scale.

Responding to Iraq's invasion of Kuwait, troops of the U.S. 1st Cavalry Division deploy across the Saudi desert during preparations prior to the Gulf War, November 4, 1990.
Greg English/The Associated Press

American soldiers surround destroyed Iraqi tanks on the blazing Burgan oil fields in Kuwait, 1991.

Bruno Barbey/Magnum Photos

Yet the U.S. military deployment in the Gulf War would rival that of Vietnam. By 1990, roughly 2 million active-duty personnel and 1.1 million reservists were serving in the U.S. armed forces. Of these, more than 500,000 would serve in the Gulf. Among those called up were 75,000 National Guard troops and reservists, the first significant mobilization of Guard units since the Korean War. Unlike Vietnam, however, the Gulf War was brief and caused few U.S. casualties. In all, 293 Americans were killed (148 in battle), with another 467 wounded.

In waging the Gulf War, President George H. W. Bush effectively secured and maintained NATO and UN backing, which meant that the economic and military burdens of the conflict were shared not only by traditional American allies but by Arab states, as well. This multilateral approach saved American lives and tax dollars while achieving carefully defined policy objectives that avoided a protracted war. Some 34 nations from six continents joined the coalition war effort, and 160,000 allied troops fought alongside U.S. forces in the Gulf. Even though American forces accounted for three-quarters of total coalition forces, American taxpayers paid only 15 percent of the war's cost, with America's allies picking up $52 billion of the war's roughly $61 billion tab.

During the massive buildup of troops in the Persian Gulf region, the Pentagon predicted that U.S. casualties in a ground war could climb as high as 30,000. "Almost six months wondering which would prevail. Peace or war. Now I knew," wrote one staff sergeant home in January 1991. "It had been a long wait, much too long. I stood there and felt sorry it had come to this, but I felt what we were doing was right. If not, God help us."

One new challenge facing the American soldier was the danger that Saddam would use chemical and biological weapons, which he had used in Iraq's war with Iran and even against Kurds in northern Iraq in 1988. Chemical-protection gear required full-body suits worn in desert temperatures reaching as high as 120 degrees. "They said that our mask will protect us against biological weapons," wrote another sergeant home, "but there is no way to tell if we are in a biological contaminated area unless someone gets sick. By the time, everyone would probably already have contaminant in them, so what good is our mask going to do?"

A record proportion of women served in the Gulf War, including 7 percent of active-duty personnel and 17 percent of National Guard and Reserve units. In the largest deployment of servicewomen in U.S. history, 35,000 were sent to the Persian Gulf (representing 6.5 percent of the forces deployed there). Although regulations forbade them from serving in ground combat roles, female soldiers performed every other duty that male soldiers performed. "I did everything from night guard during the ground war to driving an Abrams tank," wrote one female sergeant in the 79th MP Company. "They trusted my abilities, but more important was the fact that they trusted me." In all, 13 female soldiers died in the war, and two were taken as prisoners of war.

All but four of the Gulf War's 44 days of combat were devoted to the air campaign alone. This remarkable air-to-ground ratio was due in large part to significant advances in weapons and aircraft technology. Precision-guided missiles (known as "smart bombs")

A Marine patrol walks across the charred oil landscape near a burning well during a perimeter security patrol near Kuwait City, March 7, 1991.
John Gaps III/The Associated Press

enabled pinpoint accuracy in hitting targets, with few collateral civilian casualties. Stealth aircraft, which evaded enemy radar detection, saw their first wide use in bombing, reconnaissance, and ground-attack missions. Stealth bombers could strike high-value targets—targets heavily defended by anti-aircraft artillery and surface-to-air missiles— that non-stealth aircraft could not approach without risk.

For ground forces, the global positioning system (GPS) enabled maneuverability without the traditional reliance on roads and landmarks, something particularly useful in the desert. Utilizing GPS coordinates, soldiers could flag enemy targets for precision-guided artillery bombardment. Night-vision technology also had its first major test in the Gulf War. These optical systems, which could be either weapon- or helmet-mounted, offered obvious tactical advantages, especially in conventional battle conditions between massed forces.

The media's coverage of the war was likewise transformed by new technologies. Where the Vietnam War had brought televised images of war into American homes, the Gulf War delivered instantaneous satellite-fed images of war into homes all over the world. The ratings and credibility of CNN—then the lone 24-hour cable news channel—soared, while the traditional networks vastly expanded their own live coverage. But the American media in the Gulf also faced military censorship for the first time since Korea. Rather than filing extensive field reports as in Vietnam, most reporters covering the Gulf War were confined to military briefings held hundreds of miles from the battle lines. Only a few journalists were pulled from press pools and escorted to the battlefront, where they were

American soldiers of the U.S. Army 18th Artillery Corps are caught in a fierce sandstorm in February 1991.

Kenneth Jarecke/Contact Press Images

permitted to interview soldiers. Although coverage was round the clock, the media were dependent on military and government sources for information, and replays of "smart bomb" hits and cruise missile launchings became staples of television news broadcasts.

The Gulf War stemmed from the Iran-Iraq War (1980–1988), an inconclusive war of attrition that left over a million dead on both sides. Saddam's war against Iran had left him deeply indebted to the oil-rich Persian Gulf States of Saudi Arabia, Kuwait, and the United Arab Emirates, which—like Saddam and most members of his Ba'athist party— were Sunni Arab and fearful of Shi'ite Iran. But Kuwait's refusal to forgive Iraq's war debt led Saddam to invade Kuwait, intending to exploit its oil wealth to advance Iraqi power in the Middle East.

When Saddam turned his war machine on fellow Sunnis, Saudi Arabia and the exiled Kuwaiti royal family appealed to the international community. The very day that Iraq invaded Kuwait, the UN Security Council voted 14–0 to demand Iraq's immediate and unconditional withdrawal; the next day, two-thirds of the 21 Arab League states demanded the same. The United States, the European Community, Japan, and the Soviet Union embargoed Iraq, and the UN passed strict economic sanctions, tightening Iraq's diplomatic and economic isolation.

Knowing that military pressure would be necessary to protect Saudi Arabia, President Bush announced Operation Desert Shield on August 7, 1990, sending 200,000 U.S. troops to the Gulf to enforce UN sanctions. Saudi, British, and French forces joined

American Special Forces arrest Iraqi soldiers trying to flee after the liberation of Kuwait City, February 26, 1991.
Patrick Durand/Corbis Sygma

largest oil spill in history. He also torched oil wells in Kuwait, creating an inferno of flaming crude that cloaked the sky in black smoke and took seven months to extinguish.

Unable to provoke a ground war, Saddam had little besides SCUD missiles to use in Iraq's defense. These Soviet-made ballistic missiles had limited accuracy but could wreak havoc and terrorize target populations. Moreover, the allies could not be sure that Saddam would not order the missiles loaded with chemical or biological agents. As one American soldier wrote from a targeted military base in Saudi Arabia, "It's an eerie feeling to hear across the airwaves to 'don full chemical protective gear: this is NO DRILL!'" One SCUD did hit a Marine barracks near Dhahran, Saudi Arabia, on February 25, killing 28 and wounding another 100. And Saddam also launched SCUDs against Israel, hoping the Israelis would retaliate and thereby undermine Arab support for the coalition. But at U.S. urging, Israel stood down.

On February 24, coalition forces finally began their ground offensive, moving against Iraqi troops who by then had been vastly weakened and dispirited by the air campaign. The ground campaign involved two offensive thrusts: U.S. Marines, joined by Saudi and Egyptian forces, struck the Iraqi lines in Kuwait while another, highly mobile armored thrust by American, British, and French units struck far to the west, a "left hook" that outflanked the Iraqi lines and cut eastward deep inside Iraq. To the surprise of commanders, coalition forces accomplished their objectives almost immediately. Iraqi soldiers, most of whom were ill-trained conscripts unwilling to fight, surrendered in droves. The ground offensive lasted just 100 hours, with President Bush halting military operations on February 28. In the cease-fire negotiated on March 3, Iraq agreed to comply with all 12 UN resolutions.

Bush and his advisers debated whether they should leave Saddam in power or run the risk of deposing him without any viable government in place that could hold a deeply divided Iraq together. They decided that exceeding the UN's stated mission of liberating Kuwait would splinter the coalition and that a lengthy occupation might destabilize the region. A postwar containment policy was established that empowered UN inspectors to monitor and destroy Iraq's arsenals, including its missiles, chemical and biological weapons, and nuclear weapons facilities. Meanwhile, American-enforced "no fly zones" were established to protect Kurdish and Shi'ite minorities in northern and southern Iraq, respectively.

The lack of a complete and final resolution could not, however, diminish the great sense of accomplishment felt by the American armed forces. As President Bush declared, "The ghosts of Vietnam have been laid to rest beneath the sands of the Arabian desert." Yet the success of the Gulf War did not ensure Bush's reelection, nor did it fully exorcize the ghosts of Vietnam. This quick and decisive multilateral war would be followed a dozen years later by a protracted and indecisive second war in the Gulf, which America would wage with far fewer allies and without UN endorsement or NATO support.

A Florida Reserve soldier says an emotional goodbye to his family before leaving for the Gulf War zone.
Will Dickey/Florida Times Union

WAR IN AFGHANISTAN

2001 -

Being with my buds who have fought next to me in over 9 fire-fights—the bond that forms is like nothing else.
> —Sergeant Jeremy Lussi,
> 10th Mountain Division, U.S. Army,
> writing from Afghanistan, December 6, 2003

On September 11, 2001, the United States was struck by a coordinated, surprise terrorist attack that killed nearly 3,000 people and placed the American home front on a heightened state of alert not seen since the attack on Pearl Harbor. Armed with little more than box cutters and pocket knives, 19 Arab-Islamic extremists breached U.S. aviation security and hijacked four U.S. commercial airliners, of which three hit their intended targets: the twin towers of the World Trade Center in New York City and the Pentagon outside Washington, D.C. Within two hours, the attacks had brought all commercial aviation and financial markets in the United States to a complete standstill, shut down 8,300 federal buildings nationwide, caused the evacuation of all federal buildings in Washington, D.C. (including the White House and the Capitol), sent the congressional leadership into protective bunkers, and kept the president either airborne or at remote air bases for much of the day. The attack marked an unprecedented breach of America's high-tech national defense and intelligence network. The War on Terror had begun, and 25 days later the United States and its allies commenced the invasion of Afghanistan.

Soldiers from the 35th Infantry Regiment conduct a raid to search for suspected Taliban members, weapons, and materials used to make improvised explosive devices, November 9, 2004.
Spc. Jerry T. Combes/U.S. Army

As President George W. Bush vowed on September 11, the United States would "make no distinction between the terrorists who committed these acts and those who harbor them." Within days, the United States and its NATO allies linked the attacks to Al Qaeda (Arabic for "the Base"). This terrorist network was run by Osama bin Laden, a radical Sunni Islamic fundamentalist and the exiled son of a Saudi Arabian billionaire, whose hatred of the United States was widely known. Al Qaeda's base camps were burrowed deep inside Afghanistan, a country about the size of Texas with a population of 28 million.

A member of a Marine reconnaissance team, with a night-vision scope mounted on his helmet, returns to Camp Rhino in southern Afghanistan following a mission near Kandahar, December 12, 2001.
Dave Martin/Associated Press

The reasons that Afghanistan afforded sanctuary for Al Qaeda terrorists extend back to a civil war that began there in 1978—a situation intensified by the Soviet Union's invasion of the country late the following year. The Soviet-Afghan War (1979–1989) pitted Soviet and Soviet-backed Afghan forces in a brutal war against anticommunist Islamic rebels known as the Mujahadeen. These guerilla forces received enormous military aid, including advanced weapons, from the United States, funneled through neighboring Pakistan. For a decade, Soviet troops were bogged down in a costly war of attrition that was dubbed "the Soviet Vietnam." By early 1989, Soviet forces had withdrawn, and the Soviet-backed Afghan government collapsed in 1992. Following the government's fall, rebel factions divided up control of the country.

In 1996, however, a splinter faction of the Mujahadeen called the Taliban (the name means "the Students") had seized the capital of Kabul; by 1998, the Taliban had gained control over 90 percent of the country. The radical Islamic regime they established allowed Al Qaeda to establish base camps from which bin Laden's organization coordinated operations and trained operatives to carry them out. In February 1998, bin Laden issued what many analysts consider his formal declaration of war against the United States. In a fatwa (religious order), he proclaimed: "To kill Americans and their allies, both civil and military, is an individual duty of every Muslim who is able."

Indeed, in the half-decade leading up to September 11, Al Qaeda attacked several U.S. positions overseas. After the end of the first Gulf War, U.S. troops had been stationed in Kuwait and Saudi Arabia. In June 1996, a suicide car bomber struck a U.S. military base in Dhahran, Saudi Arabia, killing 19 American servicemen and injuring hundreds of others.

A U.S. soldier of the 82nd Airborne Division exits a possible ambush cave, often used by Taliban and Al Qaeda fighters, July 29, 2002.
Wally Santana/Associated Press

In August 1998, Al Qaeda launched simultaneous bomb attacks on the U.S. embassies in the capitals of Kenya and Tanzania, killing nearly a dozen American citizens and injuring hundreds of local people. This attack prompted a massive cruise-missile attack by the United States against an Al Qaeda base camp in Afghanistan, which did some damage but did not eliminate its network. In Yemen in October 2000, a suicide boat hit the destroyer *USS Cole* while it was refueling in the port city of Aden. Seventeen American sailors were killed and dozens injured. By the 2000 presidential campaign, Al Qaeda was considered a high security threat to the United States, yet neither the Republican nor the Democratic candidate raised it as a major campaign issue.

As the first military stage in the War on Terror, Operation Enduring Freedom began on October 7, 2001. Within two months, an American-led coalition, joined by an Afghan anti-Taliban group known as the Northern Alliance, dislodged the Taliban from power and destroyed the base camps of bin Laden and his Al Qaeda supporters. A new coalition government was set up under Hamid Karzai (an anti-Taliban warlord), whose fragile regime required the presence of international peacekeeping forces and enormous economic aid for reconstruction. Karzai was formally elected president of Afghanistan in October 2004, and that December the Afghan people elected a new national parliament—the first in 30 years.

◀ *Soldiers of the 19th Special Forces Group Airborne search compounds in Narizah, near Kabul. U.S. Special Forces were the first to enter villages during Operation Mountain Sweep, August 22, 2002.*
Wally Santana/The Associated Press

▲ *Soldiers with the 187th Infantry Regiment scan the nearby ridgeline for enemy movement during Operation Anaconda, March 4, 2002.*
Spc. David Marck Jr./U.S. Army

The American-led war in Afghanistan involved a broad multilateral response comparable to that of the first Gulf War. The day after the September 11 attacks, NATO for the first time invoked Article 5 of its charter, which states that an attack against one member nation is an attack against all members. This invocation was ratified on October 4, 2001, three days before the invasion of Afghanistan. UN resolutions in November 2001, moreover, condemned the Taliban for offering protective sanctuary to Al Qaeda, and in December the UN Security Council authorized the creation of the International Security Assistance Force (ISAF) to maintain security in Afghanistan. In 2003, NATO took over command of the ISAF, marking the first time that NATO assumed command of a mission beyond the North Atlantic region that the alliance was originally formed to protect. By 2007, the ISAF comprised troops from more than 30 nations.

Afghanistan's mountainous, windswept terrain and its intemperate climate—marked by blizzards in the cold winters and dust storms in the hot, dry summers—have proved challenging for those fighting there. "The only thing that changes is the wind," wrote one marine corporal in December 2001. "If there is no wind like today, it's pretty hot out here. But when the wind comes, it gets fairly cool. The wind kicks up a lot of sand." The climate's difficulties, combined with the loneliness experienced by the troops, have impacted morale. "Actually any which way you look at it, it's rough out here, but especially emotionally," added the same corporal. "Not only from the absolute isolation, both geographically and communications-wise, but from the rigors of war itself."

An army sergeant of the 102nd Infantry Regiment looks out over a valley while soldiers from his unit search for enemy observation posts and weapons caches, January 3, 2007.
Staff Sgt. Michael L. Casteel/U.S. Army

Land mines present one of the greatest threats to American ground forces in Afghanistan. After a quarter-century of warfare, an estimated 10 million mines litter much of the country's landscape, making Afghanistan one of the most heavily land-mined areas in the world. "It's only by a miracle that all my buddies are still here and alive," one sergeant wrote home in August 2003 after his men's vehicle hit a land mine. "The explosion lifted the whole 12,000 lbs armor humvee in the air. It blew the engine area up and blew the right tire to bits. Parts of which flew 800 meters." (Miraculously, none of these soldiers was seriously injured.)

As in all foreign wars marked by a prolonged presence, American soldiers have been placed in ongoing contact with the local population. Many soldiers have particularly enjoyed their interaction with Afghan children. "It was fun and they wanted everything I had," wrote the sergeant quoted above, whose men often shared candy and other gifts with the kids they encountered. On another occasion he had a chance to interact with Afghan soldiers. "We drank chi [tea] and ate hajji bread for breakfast," he wrote. "I learned how to spell my name in Arabic and got the whole alphabet down. It was pretty fun."

In the wars that have followed September 11, new and diverse communications technologies have enabled instant and frequent contact between American soldiers and their families and friends at home. While access to computers may be limited on the battlefield, the computer has revolutionized the link between soldier and citizen. Email, instant messaging, chat rooms, blogs, and digital photos have permitted soldiers to correspond

Wounded U.S. soldiers from the 10th Mountain Division are moved for evacuation after a firefight with Islamic militants. The soldiers were constructing a forward operating base in Nuristan, August 10, 2006.
Robert Nickelsberg/Getty Images

directly from the war zones, while at the same time allowing the American public to gather information about the war from sources other than media outlets and government agencies. Satellite-based communications allow soldiers to speak directly with people back home, and calling cards and cell phones now compete with the stamps and stationery of earlier wars.

The U.S. war in Afghanistan marked its sixth anniversary in October 2007, making it the third-longest American war, after Vietnam and the American Revolution. After a half-dozen years in Afghanistan, roughly 25,000 U.S. troops and 25,000 NATO forces (more than four times the number in 2003) were battling a continuing Taliban insurgency that threatened stability in Afghanistan. During this time, more than 450 U.S. service personnel had been killed (plus 250 soldiers from 18 allied nations), while another 6,700 Americans had been wounded (1,700 in action). Yet one common, enduring factor that has sustained American fighters in this long war has been the camaraderie that binds them to their fellow soldiers. "Interestingly enough," wrote one Marine colonel home in March 2002, "what keeps you going despite the fear and exhaustion are not abstractions like freedom and honor and discipline (though those are the most important). No, what really keeps you going is the guy next to you. The one counting on you to do your job, just as you are counting on him to do his."

A tearful U.S. staff sergeant in Kabul salutes during a ceremony marking the fifth anniversary of the September 11 attack on the World Trade Center, September 11, 2006.
Musadeq Sadeq/The Associated Press

Flag-draped cases containing the remains of U.S. soldiers killed in an explosion at a weapons cache near Kabul await transport home in a U.S. Air Force C-17, February 2, 2004.
Tech. Sgt. Brian Davidson/The Associated Press/U.S Air Force

IRAQ WAR

2003 -

We were from all different walks. We had a bunch of us corn-fed boys and a bunch of city guys. We had Latinos and everything else. We just bonded and became a group.
> —Specialist Cole Augustine, U.S. Army,
> writing from Iraq

On March 20, 2003, President George W. Bush ordered the invasion of Iraq. Little more than three weeks later, U.S. and British forces had occupied Iraq after a formidable air and land campaign, termed Operation Iraqi Freedom. With the fall of Baghdad on April 9, crowds of jubilant Iraqis took to the streets to celebrate the fall of Saddam Hussein's twenty-plus-year dictatorship. But Iraqis' welcome of the regime's end did not translate into a stable U.S. occupation, as formidable insurgent movements arose to challenge the post-invasion order.

Although President Bush, standing under a banner reading "Mission Accomplished" on the deck of the *USS Abraham Lincoln,* declared an end to major combat operations on May 1, 2003, American soldiers have since faced a protracted guerilla war—one for which the Pentagon was inadequately prepared and the American soldier inadequately equipped. At the time of this writing the United States was approaching the fifth anniversary of the Iraq War's start. The total U.S. death toll was expected to surpass 4,000, and the number of those wounded to exceed 30,000.

U.S. troops battle their way across a bridge amid shouted orders and heavy enemy fire in an early fight in Baghdad.
Kuni Takahashi/The Associated Press/Boston Herald

*Risking their lives to save another, Marines drag a
wounded civilian to safety after he was caught in the
midst of a battle on the road to Baghdad, 2003.*
Cheryl Diaz Meyer/The Dallas Morning News, 2004 Pulitzer Prize

With the sunlight obliterated by a heavy sandstorm, red and orange skies create an eerie and ominous welcome to troops of the 3rd Infantry Division as they advance toward Baghdad, March 2003.
David Leeson/The Dallas Morning News, 2004 Pulitzer Prize

The road to war in Iraq began in January 2002, with President Bush's first State of the Union address after the September 11 attacks. Outlining what his administration saw as obstacles to winning the War on Terror, he labeled Iraq (along with North Korea and Iran) part of the "Axis of Evil." In a speech before the UN that September, Bush referred to Iraq under Saddam as "a grave and gathering danger" and warned that if the UN failed to enforce its resolutions requiring Iraq to disclose its weapons of mass destruction (WMDs) and to disarm itself of them, then the United States and its "coalition of the willing" would act militarily without UN mandate. Despite the renewal of the UN weapons inspection program and the containment of Iraq through existing economic sanctions and military "no-fly" zones, however, the Bush administration—backed by the government of British prime minister Tony Blair—laid out a case for preemptive war.

The Bush administration concluded that the 12-year containment policy against Iraq had failed and that the reinvigorated UN inspections were futile given Saddam's obstructionist track record. "Simply stated," warned Vice President Dick Cheney in August 2002, "there is no doubt that Saddam Hussein now has weapons of mass destruction. There is no doubt he is amassing them to use against our friends, against our allies, and against us." In October 2002, Congress passed a resolution granting the president authority to use force against Iraq, with the House voting 296–133 and the Senate 77–23. In the wake of the invasion, however, a 1,400-member international team led by the Pentagon and CIA failed to find any WMDs in Iraq. Many experts believed that the UN's disarmament program, which had commenced after the first Gulf War, had succeeded in eliminating them.

An American soldier of the 37th Armored Regiment patrols a residential street in Tall Afar while a young Iraqi girl walks beside him, August 13, 2006.

Staff Sgt. Jacob N. Bailey/U.S. Air Force

The Iraq War has so far had two stages: the invasion (March 20–April 30, 2003), followed by the occupation and an insurgency campaign that was continuing nearly half a decade later. During the invasion stage, 139 American military personnel were killed—less than half the number of American fatalities suffered during the first Gulf War. Of the 300,000 coalition forces engaged in the invasion of Iraq in March 2003, 98 percent were American or British, including 250,000 American personnel (160,000 ground troops) and 45,000 British forces. While this strength proved more than capable of quickly overwhelming the Iraqi Army on the battlefield, the numbers proved insufficient to handle the guerilla insurgency that ensued.

The insurgency drew battle lines in the streets of Iraqi cities and towns, blurring distinctions between civilians and combatants. To counter U.S. forces' superior technological advantages, insurgents often relied on a myriad of improvised explosive devices (IEDs), also known as roadside bombs. These proved the insurgents' most lethal weapons, causing more than a third of all American casualties in Iraq. Initial U.S. war plans predicting an occupation force of only 30,000 to 50,000 by the end of 2003 were overly optimistic and shortsighted. By the fall of 2007, 168,000 U.S. troops were stationed in Iraq—up from the approximately 130,000 U.S. troops deployed there in June 2006.

▲ *Soldiers of the army's 101st Airborne Division fire a TOW missile at a building in Mosul suspected of harboring Saddam Hussein's sons, July 22, 2003.*
Sgt. Curtis G. Hargrave/U.S. Army

▶ *A badly wounded Marine, who had used his body to shield another Marine from a grenade, is carried out of a house in Fallujah, November 13, 2004.*
Lucian Read/WPN

◀ *After three weeks and 300-plus miles of speed-and-maneuver warfare, a sergeant on the road to Baghdad savors the first letters from his wife, 2003.*
Cheryl Diaz Meyer/The Dallas Morning News, 2004 Pulitzer Prize

▼ *Members of the 82nd Airborne take a much-needed rest along the Syrian border before their next mission, November 21, 2003.*
Joseph White

Female soldiers have played an essential role in the Iraq conflict. Women now make up 14 percent—or one in seven—of all active-duty personnel in the U.S. military, and women officers have risen to the highest levels of command. By the 2000s, female soldiers were allowed to perform nearly all the duties of their male counterparts. Although still officially prohibited from serving in combat units, female soldiers are, in fact, often engaged in fighting, and a significant number have become casualties of war. By the summer of 2007, more than 80 female soldiers had been killed and more than 450 wounded in Iraq. A total of 160,000 women had served the armed forces in Iraq and Afghanistan—an enormous increase over the 35,000 who served in the Gulf War and the 7,500 in Vietnam.

Meanwhile, immigrant soldiers had become increasingly important in filling the ranks of the U.S. armed forces. By 2006, nearly 70,000 foreign-born men and women were in uniform, representing 5 percent of total active-duty personnel. Two out of five were not U.S. citizens but rather lawful permanent residents (with "green card" status).

A Marine assists his buddy, who was shot by a sniper in fighting at Karma. While under attack, the Marine pulled his comrade out of the line of fire and treated his wound, November 2006.
Joao Silva/The New York Times

A baby greets his aunt for the first time at the soldier's homecoming in Sacramento, California. The sergeant had served 15 months in Iraq.

Renee C. Byer/The Associated Press/Sacramento Bee

"I knew we'd be going to war, and I wanted to help this country that had given me and my family opportunity," said one female immigrant soldier who served a tour in Iraq. Having come to the United States from Mexico in 1993, she added, "I feel like an American, and now I want to be a citizen, to have my complete rights, to vote, and be part of the system." Before enlisting, non-citizen soldiers must pass an English-language proficiency test and an extensive criminal background check; given this more thorough vetting process, they have lower attrition rates than citizen soldiers.

Like the first Gulf War, the war in Iraq has required American soldiers to adjust to harsh desert conditions. But the earlier engagement in the Persian Gulf region was very brief, and American troops have not fought in such conditions for an extended time since the North Africa campaign of World War II. The intense summer heat is especially difficult to endure. "You get to being so hot with all the gear on and the heat that you're ready to black out," wrote one lance corporal, "but I'm becoming used to it. It's almost funny, the heat dropped to 90 degrees one night and I needed a sleeping bag!" Sandstorms, which can suddenly erase visibility and bring movement to a halt, are also a challenge. "It was just after noon and it was almost dark," wrote another lance corporal who participated in the initial invasion. "The sky was completely orange—you couldn't see more than 30 feet in front of you. It was insane."

Between 2001 and 2007, 1.5 million Americans served in the armed forces in Iraq and Afghanistan, with nearly 450,000 serving multiple extended tours (now 15 months long). Some troops have been given only a few months "dwell time" stateside before being redeployed, and another 70,000 troops have been held on active duty beyond their contracted service commitments. This situation has placed especially grave demands on National Guard and Reserve units, who by 2005 made up nearly 50 percent of troops serving in Iraq. Personnel shortages required levels of duty not seen since World War II—even as the Pentagon, in an effort to boost recruitment, lowered the enlistment age, reduced education and aptitude standards, and increased enlistment bonuses.

As this book went to press, debate continued about whether to withdraw U.S. troops from Iraq—forcing the Iraqi government to assume sole responsibility for containing the insurgency—or to prolong the U.S. military presence there to ensure Iraq's stability. By some estimates, achieving that stability might require a commitment for years to come. Either way, the American soldier will continue to carry the burden of protecting America's strategic interests as defined by policymakers and voters. Certainly, American soldiers in Iraq share a common bond with American soldiers in every war. One 23-year-old corporal summed it up best in a letter he wrote to his parents from Iraq in April 2003: "I know I don't say it enough but I love you more than anything in this world and I would do anything for you. I'm glad I joined the Marine Corps, also that I could make you so proud of me, because that's all I want is for you guys to be able to say 'That is our son' with pride."

Arts and Humanities References

CIVIL WAR

History, Memoirs, Fiction, and Poetry

Louisa May Alcott. *Civil War Hospital Sketches.* 1863; reprint, Mineola, N.Y.: Dover Publications, 2006. Alcott's sketches are based on her experiences as a Civil War nurse.

Ambrose Bierce. *Civil War Stories.* Mineola, N.Y.: Dover Publications, 1994. The volume includes Bierce's classic stories "An Occurrence at Owl Creek Bridge," "Four Days in Dixie," and "What I Saw of Shiloh," originally published in *Tales of Soldiers and Civilians,* 1891.

Claudius Meade Capps, ed. *The Blue and the Gray: The Best Poems of the Civil War.* Freeport, N.Y.: Books for Libraries Press, 1943. The anthology includes works by John Greenleaf Whittier, Walt Whitman, Julia Ward Howe, Herman Melville, William Cullen Bryant, Francis Scott Key, and Bret Harte, among others.

Stephen Crane. *The Red Badge of Courage.* 1894. Many editions are currently available.

Kathleen Diffley, ed. *To Live and Die: Collected Stories of the Civil War, 1861–1876.* Durham, N.C.: Duke University Press, 2002.

Shelby Foote, ed. *Chickamauga, and Other Civil War Stories.* New York: Delta, 1993.

Ellen Glasgow. *The Battleground.* New York: Doubleday Page, 1902. Long out of print, the book is available through online secondhand book sellers.

Mary Johnston. *Cease Firing.* 1912; reprint, Baltimore: Johns Hopkins University Press, 1996.

Mary Johnston. *The Long Roll.* 1911; reprint, Baltimore: Johns Hopkins University Press, 1996.

Sidney Lanier. *Tiger-Lilies: A Novel,* 1866; reprint, Chapel Hill, N.C.: University of North Carolina Press, 1969. The entire text of the novel can be found on line, at http://etext.lib.virginia.edu/etcbin/eafbin2/toccer-eaf?id=Leaf629&tag=public&data=/www/data/eaf2/private/texts&part=0.

Louis P. Masur. *". . . the real war will never get in the books": Selections from Writers during the Civil War.* New York: Oxford University Press, 1993.

Herman Melville. *Battle Pieces.* 1866; reprint, Edison, N.J.: Castle Books, 2000.

William Gilmore Simms, ed. *War Poetry of the South.* 1866; reprint, Ann Arbor, Mich.: Scholarly Publishing Office, University of Michigan Library, 2005.

Harriet Beecher Stowe. *Uncle Tom's Cabin.* 1852. Many editions are currently available.

Mark Twain. *Merry Tales.* 1892; reprint, New York: Oxford University Press, 1996. The collection includes Twain's antiwar story "The Private History of a Campaign That Failed."

Jules Verne. *Texar's Revenge, or North Against South.* 1887 (originally published in French); reprint of English translation, N.p.: Fredonia Books, 2002.

Walt Whitman. *Drum Taps.* 1865; reprint, Whitefish, Mont.: Kessinger Publishing, 2004. This collection of poetry is based on Whitman's time as a psychological nurse in the hospitals of Washington, D.C. A complete gathering of all of Whitman's Civil War poems is on the Web, at http://members.tripod.com/~DizzyDi2/.

Online Literature Resource

www.civilwarliterature.com. The site provides access to Civil War stories drawn from the pages of *Harper's Weekly* magazine, as well as news articles, illustrations, cartoons, and commentary from the period.

Theater

Walter J. Meserve and Mollie Ann Meserve, eds. *Fateful Lightning: American Civil War Plays.* New York: Feedback & Prospero, 2000. The collection includes *Uncle Tom's Cabin* and *Ossawattomie Brown.*

Movies and Television

The Birth of a Nation (1915), directed by D. W. Griffith; adapted from Thomas Dixon's novel *The Clansman.* Controversial from the time of its release, Griffith's film remains a classic of early American cinema despite its white supremacist slant.

Their One Love (1915), directed by Jack Harvey. This early film includes spectacular nighttime battle scenes.

The General (1927), directed by Buster Keaton and Clyde Bruckman. Keaton also stars in this silent-film comedy.

Abraham Lincoln (1930), directed by D. W. Griffith.

Gone With the Wind (1939), directed by Victor Fleming. Starring Vivien Leigh and Clark Gable, this Academy Award–winning film was based on the bestselling 1936 novel by Margaret Mitchell.

Glory (1989), directed by Edward Zwick. *Glory* tells the story of the 54th Regiment of the Massachusetts Volunteer Infantry, the first unit of African-American soldiers to fight for the Union cause under commanding officer Robert Gould Shaw. The screenplay was based on Shaw's letters.

The Civil War (1990), directed by Ken Burns. This multi-episode survey of the war, produced for PBS, set a new standard for television documentaries.

Gettysburg (1993), directed by Ronald F. Maxwell. This four-and-a-half-hour movie includes some of the most authentic reenactments of the battle.

Cold Mountain (2003), directed by Anthony Minghella. The film was adapted from the bestselling 1997 novel by Charles Frazier, which was loosely based on the experiences of Frazier's ancestor William Pinkney Inman, a Civil War private.

Music

Richard Crawford. *The Civil War Songbook: Complete Original Sheet Music for 37 Songs.* Mineola, N.Y.: Dover Publications, 1977.

Col. Rick Richardson, narration and vocals. *Songs of the Civil War.* The recording includes "Shilo," "Pride of Battery B," "Hard Times," "The Rebel Soldier," "Two Little Boys," "Lorinna," "The Tupelo Brigade," "The Dying Rebel's Plea," "Dixie Forever," and "Southern Man." To order the cassette, send $13.19 to Rick Richardson, 3059 Jones Loop, Terry, MS 39170.

Online Music Resources

www.artsedge.kennedy-center.org/content/2095/. This Web page presents a Civil War music lesson plan developed by ArtsEdge, the National Arts and Education Network (a program of the Kennedy Center in Washington, D.C.).

www.authentichistory.com/civilwar/sounds/index.html. The site features early-20th century recordings of Civil War era songs, including "The Battle Hymn of the Republic" and "When Johnny Comes Marching Home."

www.civilwarpoetry.org. Besides poetry, the site contains lyrics to scores of songs popular during the Civil War.

Visual Arts

Hermann Warner Williams, Jr. *The Civil War: the Artists' Record.* Boston: Beacon Press, 1961. This catalog of an exhibition mounted at Washington, D.C.'s Corcoran Gallery and Boston's Museum of Fine Arts, though out of print, is available through online secondhand book sellers.

Stephen W. Sears. *Civil War: A Treasury of Art and Literature.* Westport, Conn.: Hugh Lauter Levin Associates, 1992.

Online Visual Arts Resource

www.loc.gov/exhibits/treasures/trm041.html. This online exhibit, part of the Library of Congress's American Treasures series, presents the battlefield drawings of Alfred Waud, an artist who worked at the front lines, sketching battle scenes for the national pictorial press.

SPANISH-AMERICAN WAR

History, Memoirs, and Contemporary Accounts

Theodore Roosevelt. *The Rough Riders/An Autobiography.* Edited by Louis Auchincloss. New York: Library of America, 2004.

R. W. Stallman. *The War Dispatches of Stephen Crane.* Edited by E. R. Hagemann. Westport, Conn.: Greenwood Publishing Group, 1977. Most famous for his Civil War novel *The Red Badge of Courage,* Crane served as a war correspondent during the Spanish-American War.

T. G. Steward. *Buffalo Soldiers: The Colored Regulars in the United States Army.* Amherst, N.Y.: Humanity Press, 2003.

Mark Twain. *Mark Twain's Weapons of Satire: Anti-Imperialist Writings on the Philippine-American War.* Edited by Jim Zwick. Syracuse, N.Y.: Syracuse University Press, 1992. Twain was a member of the Anti-Imperialist League; his sentiments about the war in the Philippines were published nationwide.

Movies and Television

The Rough Riders (1927; silent), directed by Victor Fleming.

Rough Riders (1997), directed by John Milius. This Emmy Award–winning made-for-TV movie starred Sam Elliot, Gary Busey, and Tom Berenger (as Teddy Roosevelt).

Online Film Resource

http://memory.loc.gov/ammem/sawhtml/sawhome.html. Film was first used for propaganda purposes during the Spanish-American War. This Web site, The Spanish-American War in Motion Pictures, is part of the Library of Congress's American Memory project. It features 68 short films from the period; all are downloadable. Included are gems such as *Love and War,* an 1899 "picture song" by the Thomas A. Edison studio; the short silent film, which was intended to be shown while a song of the same title was played and sung, follows a soldier going to war, fighting bravely, falling in love with a Red Cross nurse, and then returning home victoriously. Not all the films are fiction: Some were shot on site and depict the actualities of conflict.

Music

At the time of the Spanish-American War, popular music was sold primarily as sheet music for the piano and parlor singing, although the public could also hear the music on early gramophone recordings. New York's Tin Pan Alley began evolving during this era, and ragtime, a forerunner of jazz, was becoming popular in the late 1890s. The song "(There'll Be) A Hot Time in the Old Town Tonight," probably written by Joe Hayden and Theodore A. Metz, was very popular during the Spanish-American War and a favorite of Roosevelt's Rough Riders; Spanish soldiers in Cuba heard the song so often that some thought it was the American national anthem! Other popular songs of the period included John Philip Sousa's marches "Stars and Stripes Forever," "El Capitan March," and "Washington Post March," as well as "Brave Dewey and His Men (Down at Manila Bay)," by E. F. Galvin and T. M. Kane, and "The Charge of the Roosevelt Riders," by Charles Coleman, both of which celebrated American victories abroad.

Online Music Resource

http://www.pbs.org/crucible/frames/_music.html. This page, part of the Web site for the PBS film *Crucible of Empire,* presents sheet music from the Spanish-American War era.

Visual Arts

Douglas Allen. *Frederic Remington and the Spanish-American War.* New York: Crown, 1971.

Online Visual Arts Resource

www.loc.gov/exhibits/treasures/trm121.html. By 1898, news photography had almost completely replaced on-site sketching as the means for conveying pictures of the battle front to readers back home. But this page, part of the Library of Congress's American Treasures site, presents sketches of Spanish-American War skirmishes by artist William Glackens (who later gained fame as a member of New York's "Ashcan" School of painters). Glackens was sent to Cuba to cover the war for *McClure's Magazine.*

BOXER REBELLION

History, Memoirs, and Fiction

Johan Gunnar Anderson. *The Dragon and the Foreign Devils.* Boston: Little, Brown, 1928.

Robert Coltman, Jr. *Beleaguered in Peking: The Boxer's War against the Foreigner.* 1901; reprint, Whitefish, Mont.: Kessinger Publishing, 2007. The author was an American doctor living in Peking during the siege.

Sarah Pike Conger. *Letters from China, with Particular Reference to the Empress Dowager and the Women of China*. 1909; reprint, Xerox University Microfilms, 1975.

Eva Jane Price. *China Journal 1889–1900: An American Missionary Family During the Boxer Rebellion*. New York: Scribner, 1989.

Lin Yutang. *Moment in Peking*. New York: John Day Company, 1939. The novel opens during the Boxer Rebellion, providing a view of the turmoil through the eyes of the young protagonist.

Movies

Foreign Devils (1927; silent), directed by W. S. Van Dyke.

55 Days at Peking (1963), directed by Nicholas Ray. This Hollywood costume epic starred Charlton Heston, Ava Gardner, and David Niven.

Boxer Rebellion (1975), directed by the Chang Cheh (Shaw Brothers studio, Hong Kong). This big-budget martial arts film (Chinese title: *Pa kuo lien chun*) tells the story of the uprising from the Chinese perspective.

Visual Arts

Frederic Sharf. *The Boxer Rebellion, China 1900: The Artists' Perspective*. London: Greenhill Books, 2006. The Boxer Rebellion was illustrated by artists from around the globe.

WORLD WAR I

History, Memoirs, Fiction, and Poetry

Pat Barker. "Regeneration" trilogy: *Regeneration* (New York: Plume, 1993), *The Eye in the Door* (New York: Plume, 1995), and *The Ghost Road* (New York: Plume, 1996).

Willa Cather. *One of Ours*. 1922; reprint, N.p.: Classic Publishers, 1998.

Humphrey Cobb. *Paths of Glory*. 1935; reprint, Athens, Ga.: University of Georgia Press, 1987.

John Dos Passos. *Three Soldiers*. 1921; reprinted in John Dos Passos, *Novels, 1920–1925,* New York: Library of America, 2003.

Niall Ferguson. *The Pity of War: Explaining World War I*. New York: Basic Books, 2000.

Ernest Hemingway. *A Farewell to Arms*. 1929; paperback ed., New York: Scribner, 1995.

Vicente Blasco Ibáñez. *The Four Horsemen of the Apocalypse*. 1919; reprint of English translation by Charlotte Brewster Jordan, Rockville, Md.: Borgo Press (Wildside), 2002.

Wilfred Owen. *The Collected Poems of Wilfred Owen*. Rev. ed, New York: New Directions, 1965.

Robert W. Service. *Rhymes of a Red Cross Man*. 1916. Several editions of Service's war poems are currently in print, and the entire text of the book is available on line, at http://etext.lib.virginia.edu/toc/modeng/public/SerRhym.html.

Siegfried Sassoon. *The War Poems of Siegfried Sassoon*. N.p.: Dodo Press, 2007.

Jon Stallworthy. *Great Poets of World War I: Poetry from the Great War*. New York: Carroll & Graf, 2002.

Gertrude Stein. *The Autobiography of Alice B. Toklas*. 1932; New York: Modern Library, 1993. Though it covers a much longer period in the life of the author and her companion, the *Autobiography* provides charming reminiscences of Stein's and Toklas's war work with the American Fund for French Wounded and of their encounters with American doughboys stationed in France.

Edward Streeter. *Dere Mable: Love Letters of a Rookie.* 1918. This comic novel's story is told in a series of egregiously misspelled letters from "Private Bill" to his sweetheart back home. It was later (1920) made into a musical comedy, with music by George Gershwin. The novel's complete text (with original illustrations) is available on line, at http://net.lib.byu.edu/estu/wwi/comment/DereMable/Mable.htm.

Dalton Trumbo. *Johnny Got His Gun.* 1939; reprint, New York: Citadel, 2007.

Ella Wheeler Wilcox. *Hello, Boys!* Wilcox's poems are available on line at Project Gutenberg, www.gutenberg.org/etext/6666.

Theater

R. C. Sherriff. *Journey's End.* 1928; reprint, New York: Penguin Modern Classics, 2000.

Agnes Cardinal. *War Plays by Women: An International Anthology.* London and New York: Routledge, 1999. Most of the plays in this anthology concern World War I.

Movies

Civilization (1916; silent), directed by Reginald Barker and Thomas H. Ince. This film, a call for pacifism, portrayed the madness of war in a mythical kingdom.

The Little American (1917; silent), directed by Cecil B. DeMille. Mary Pickford starred in this propagandistic drama about a young American woman whose ship is torpedoed by a German U-boat.

Hearts of the World (1918; silent), directed by D. W. Griffith. A collaboration between the British government and American filmmaker Griffith, the film features scenes filmed in France and includes uncredited appearances by some of the era's biggest stars, including Lilian Gish and Noel Coward.

Shoulder Arms (1918; silent), directed by Charles Chaplin. Chaplin plays a dreaming soldier in this comedy set in wartime France.

The Four Horsemen of the Apocalypse (1921; silent), directed by Rex Ingram. Based on the 1919 novel by Vicente Blasco Ibáñez, the film uses the horrors of the war as a background for a tragic love story.

The Big Parade (1925; silent), directed by King Vidor. This film is considered the first realistic motion picture about war.

Wings (1927; silent), directed by William A. Wellman. The film, which tells the story of two fighter pilots, was the only silent movie ever to win the Academy Award for Best Picture.

All Quiet on the Western Front (1930), directed by Lewis Milestone. Based on the 1929 novel by Erich Maria Remarque, the film offers a devastating look at the horrors of war through the eyes of a young soldier.

Hell's Angels (1930), directed by Howard Hughes. This movie about two brothers who join the Royal Air Force contains breathtaking scenes of World War I air battles—and features Jean Harlow's first film appearance.

A Farewell to Arms (1932), directed by Frank Borzage. Based on Hemingway's 1929 novel, the film stars Gary Cooper.

Sergeant York (1941), directed by Howard Hawks. Another Gary Cooper vehicle, the film is based on the World War I journal of Alvin Cullum York, who began the war as a pacifist but went on to win the Congressional Medal of Honor for his bravery in combat.

Paths of Glory (1957), directed by Stanley Kubrick. Based on the 1935 novel by Humphrey Cobb and starring Kirk Douglas, the film is widely considered one of the most powerful antiwar movies ever made.

Johnny Got His Gun (1971), directed by Dalton Trumbo. Based on his own novel of three decades earlier, Trumbo made this movie as a protest against the Vietnam War. It tells the story of a badly wounded soldier in 1918.

Music

The World War I years saw an outpouring of patriotic and sentimental songs, including "Over There" (1917), by George M. Cohan; "It's a Long, Long Way to Tipperary" (1914), by Arthur Fields and Jack Judge; "Pack Up Your Troubles In Your Old Kit Bag" (1916), by Felix Powell and George Asaf; "Till We Meet Again" (1918), by Raymond Egan and Richard Whiting; "Hinky Dinky Parlay Vous" (1924), sheet music by Jimmy McHugh; "Keep the Home Fires Burning" (1916), by Ivor Novello and Lena Guilbert Ford; and, perhaps most famous, "God Bless America" (1918), by Irving Berlin.

Visual Arts

Richard Cork. *A Bitter Truth: Avant-Garde Art and the Great War.* New Haven: Yale University Press, 1994.

Peter Krass. *Portrait of War: The U.S. Army's First Combat Artists and the Doughboys' Experience in WWI.* Hoboken, N.J.: John Wiley, 2006. The book tells the story of the first combat artists recruited by the army.

Online Visual Arts Resources

www.art-ww1.com/gb/present.html. This Web site, entitled "Art of the First World War," was mounted in 1998 to commemorate the 80th anniversary of the war's end; it displays 100 works—including political posters—by European and American artists of the period.

www.worldwar1.com/posters.htm. This site displays propaganda posters from all the combatant nations of World War I.

WORLD WAR II

Fiction

William Faulkner. "Two Soldiers" (short story). 1942; reprinted in *The Selected Short Stories of William Faulkner* (New York: Modern Library, 1993).

Joseph Heller. *Catch-22.* 1961; paperback ed., New York: Vintage, 1994.

James Jones. *From Here to Eternity.* 1953; reprint, New York: Gramercy, 2004.

James Jones. *The Thin Red Line.* 1962; reprint, 1998, available through Amazon Remainders (Amazon.com).

Norman Mailer. *The Naked and the Dead.* 1948; 50th anniversary edition, New York: Picador, 2000.

Irwin Shaw. *The Young Lions.* 1948; reprint with foreword by James Salter, Chicago: University of Chicago Press, 2000.

Herman Wouk. *The Winds of War.* 1971; paperback ed., N.p.: Back Bay Books, 2002.

Herman Wouk. *War and Remembrance.* 1978; reprinted in various editions since its first publication.

Theater

Maxwell Anderson. *Candle in the Wind*. 1941; out of print.

Lillian Hellman. *Watch on the Rhine*. 1941; reprinted in *Six Plays by Lillian Hellman* (New York: Vintage, 1979).

Arthur Laurents. *Home of the Brave*. 1945; reprint, New York: Dramatists Play Service, 1998.

Cole Porter. *Something for the Boys*. 1943; the original radio cast recording, starring Ethel Merman, was reissued, on CD, in 1995.

Albert Wertheim. *Staging the War: American Drama and World War II*. Bloomington, Ind.: Indiana University Press, 2003.

Movies

World War II has inspired filmmakers like no other war. From the war's earliest years until the present, moviemakers have responded by creating films on every aspect of this global conflict. What follows is a very incomplete listing of movies about the war, most chosen for inclusion here because of their focus on the American soldier. (A few other classic World War II films are also included.)

Across the Pacific (1942), directed by John Huston.

Casablanca (1942), directed by Michael Curtiz.

Flying Tigers (1942), directed by David Miller.

Mrs. Miniver (1942), directed by William Wyler.

Bataan (1943), directed by Tay Garnett.

Destination Tokyo (1943), directed by Delmer Daves.

This Is the Army (1943), directed by Michael Curtiz; based on two Broadway shows by Irving Berlin. This musical review features performances by actual soldiers, as well as Kate Smith singing "God Bless America."

Thirty Seconds Over Tokyo (1944), directed by Mervyn LeRoy.

Winged Victory (1944), directed by George Cukor; based on the play by Moss Hart.

The Story of G.I. Joe (1945), directed by William Wellman.

They Were Expendable (1945), directed by John Ford.

The Best Years of Our Lives (1946), directed by William Wyler.

From Here to Eternity (1953), directed by Fred Zinneman; based on the novel by James Jones.

Stalag 17 (1953), directed by Billy Wilder.

Mister Roberts (1955), directed by John Ford and Mervyn LeRoy.

To Hell and Back (1955), directed by Jessie Hibbs.

The Man in the Gray Flannel Suit (1956), directed by Nunnally Johnson.

The Bridge on the River Kwai (1957), directed by David Lean.

The Naked and the Dead (1958), directed by Raoul Walsh; based on the novel by Norman Mailer.

South Pacific (1958), directed by Joshua Logan; based on the hit Broadway musical by Rodgers and Hammerstein.

The Young Lions (1958), directed by Edward Dmytryk; based on the novel by Irwin Shaw.

The Longest Day (1962), directed by Ken Annakin and Andrew Marton.

The Battle of the Bulge (1965), directed by Ken Annakin.

The Dirty Dozen (1967), directed by Robert Aldrich.

Catch-22 (1970), directed by Mike Nichols; based on the novel by Joseph Heller.

Patton (1970), directed by Franklin J. Schaffner.

A Midnight Clear (1992), directed by Keith Gordon.

Saving Private Ryan (1998), directed by Steven Spielberg.

The Thin Red Line (1998), directed by Terrence Malick; based on the novel by James Jones.

Pearl Harbor (2001), directed by Michael Bay.

Two Soldiers (2003), directed by Aaron Schneider; based on the short story by William Faulkner.

Flags of Our Fathers (2006), directed by Clint Eastwood.

Television

Television, too, has often drawn inspiration from World War II. Here are a few of the series, miniseries, and documentaries about the war that have appeared on American TV:

McHale's Navy (1962–1966); comedy series.

Combat! (1962–1967); dramatic series.

Hogan's Heroes (1965–1971); comedy series.

The Winds of War (1983), directed by Dan Curtis; miniseries based on the Herman Wouk novel.

War and Remembrance (1988), directed by Dan Curtis and Tommy Groszman; miniseries based on the Herman Wouk novel.

Band of Brothers (2001), directed by David Frankel, Tom Hanks, and others; dramatic miniseries, written by historian Stephen Ambrose and based on interviews with members of Easy Company, of the U.S. Army's 101st airborne division, as well as on soldiers' journals and letters.

The War (2007), directed by Ken Burns and Lynn Novick; a multi-episode PBS documentary.

Movies and Television Resources

Robert L. McLaughlin and Sally E. Parry. *We'll Always Have the Movies: American Cinema during World War II.* Lexington, Ky.: University Press of Kentucky, 2006.

www.lib.berkeley.edu/MRC/Warfilm.html. The Web site, from the University of California at Berkeley library, offers an extensive listing of World War II films.

Music

Before and during World War II, the United States became a haven for European composers and musicians including Béla Bartók, George Szell, Arnold Schoenberg, and Kurt Weill. Big bands dominated the popular music of the period. Much of the popular music of World War II, like that of World War I, was patriotic and upbeat or sentimental. Hits included "The Boogie Woogie Bugle Boy of Company B" (1941), recorded by the Andrews Sisters; "G. I. Jive" (1939), by Johnny Mercer; "This Land is Your Land" (1940), by Woody Guthrie; "Remember Pearl Harbor" (1941), by Don Reid and Sammy Kaye; and "Back Home for Keeps" (1945), by Bob Russell and Carmen Lombardo. An illustrated songbook of the war years, *I'll Be Seeing You: 51 Songs of World War II*, was published in 1995 by the Hal Leonard Corporation of Milwaukee. Available collections of recordings include the following:

Remember Pearl Harbor: Songs That Won the War (Varese Sarabande, 2001).

The Words and Music of World War II (Sony, 1991).

Visual Arts

Many European artists fled Hitler for the United States during WWII. They included Max Ernst, Max Beckman, and George Grosz. Resources on art made during World War II include these:

Ellen Landau. *Artists for Victory: An Exhibition Catalogue.* Washington, D.C.: U.S. Government Printing Office, 1983.

Barbara McCloskey. *Artists of World War II.* Westport, Conn.: Greenwood, 2005.

KOREAN WAR

Fiction, Poetry, and Journalism

Thomas Anderson. *Your Own Beloved Sons.* New York: Random House, 1956.

Gene L. Coon. *Meanwhile, Back at the Front.* New York: Crown, 1961.

W. D. Ehrhart & Philip K. Jason, eds. *Retrieving Bones: Stories and Poems of the Korean War.* New Brunswick, N.J.: Rutgers University Press, 1999.

Charles Bracelen Flood. *More Lives Than One.* Boston: Houghton Mifflin, 1967.

Pat Frank. *Hold Back the Night.* Philadelphia: Lippincott, 1952.

Edward Herbert Franklin. *It's Cold in Pongo-ni.* New York: Vanguard, 1965.

James Hickey. *Chrysanthemum in the Snow: The Novel of the Korean War.* New York: Crown, 1990.

Richard E. Kim. *The Martyred.* New York: George Braziller, 1964.

Michael Lynch. *An American Soldier.* Boston: Little, Brown, 1969.

Bill Mauldin. *Bill Mauldin in Korea.* New York: Norton, 1952. Journalist and cartoonist Bill Mauldin created G.I. Joe during WWII, when he was a soldier. He returned to the war in Korea as a journalist.

Francis Pollini. *Night.* Boston: Houghton Mifflin, 1961.

George Sidney. *For the Love of Dying.* New York: William Morrow, 1969.

William Styron. *The Long March.* 1952; reprint, New York: Vintage Classics, 2001.

Theater

Henry Denker and Ralph Berkey. *Time Limit!* New York: Samuel French, 1956. This Broadway play concerned the POW collaboration issue.

Movies and Television

Fixed Bayonets (1951), directed by Samuel Fuller. The film relates the story of U.S. soldiers in Korea surviving the harsh winter of 1951.

The Steel Helmet (1951), directed by Samuel Fuller. Released shortly after the war started, this first Korean War combat film remains one of the better treatments of the conflict.

The Bridges at Toko-Ri (1954), directed by Mark Robson. From the 1953 book by James A. Michener, the movie tells the story of a U.S. Navy Reserve pilot flying attack missions over North Korea.

Target Zero (1955), directed by Harmon Jones. The movie depicts U.S., British, and South Korean troops trapped behind enemy lines.

Battle Hymn (1956), directed by Douglas Sirk. The movie, starring Rock Hudson, is based on the autobiography of Col. Dean E. Hess, an American clergyman and veteran World War II fighter pilot who volunteered to return to active duty to train the fighter pilots of the South Korean Air Force.

The Rack (1956), directed by Arnold Laven. Written by Rod Serling, the film stars Paul Newman as a repatriated Korean War POW.

Men in War (1957), directed by Anthony Mann. This action-packed Korean War drama makes the point that combat is fundamentally a nasty business of attrition and survival.

The Hunters (1958), directed by Dick Powell. The film is an adaptation of the 1956 novel by James Salter, himself an F-86 pilot in the Korean War.

Pork Chop Hill (1959), directed by Lewis Milestone. This realistic film about an infantry company given the task of taking an important hill in the Iron Triangle north of Seoul was adapted from the 1956 book by S. L. A. Marshall.

All the Young Men (1960), directed by Hall Bartlett. The film, which deals with racial desegregation in the army, stars Sidney Poitier.

The Manchurian Candidate (1962), directed by John Frankenheimer. In this film adapted from the 1959 novel by Richard Condon, the principal characters are captured and brainwashed during the Korean War.

M.A.S.H. (1970), directed by Robert Altman. Altman's dark comedy, based on the books *MASH: An Army Surgeon in Korea,* by Otto F. Apel, Jr., and *MASH: A Novel of Three Army Doctors,* by Richard Hooker, inspired the long-running (1972–1983) TV sitcom *M*A*S*H,* featuring Alan Alda.

Online Music Resource

http://nwfolk.com/songlists/korean_war.html. This Web site contains a listing of folk songs and other songs inspired by the Korean War.

Visual Arts

H. Avery Chenoweth. *Art of War: Eyewitness U.S. Combat Art from the Revolution through the Twentieth Century.* New York: Friedman/Fairfax (Barnes and Noble), 2004. Col. Chenoweth was a Marine combat artist in Korea, Vietnam, and the Gulf War; his interesting text fleshes out the stories of the combat artists, their backgrounds, and their war experiences.

The Korean War in American Art & Culture: Fifty Years Later. East Hampton, N.Y.: Guild Hall Museum, 2000. (Exhibition catalog.)

Online Visual Arts Resource

www.authentichistory.com/1950s/koreanwar/index.html. This Web site features images from comic books from the Korean War era, providing visual images of soldiers, uniforms, and weaponry, as well as stories from the front.

VIETNAM WAR

Fiction, Memoirs, and Poetry

John Balaban. *After Our War.* Pittsburgh: University of Pittsburgh Press, 1974. (poetry)

D. C. Berry. *Saigon Cemetery.* Athens, Ga.: University of Georgia Press, 1972. (poetry)

Dennis Phillip Caron. *Eagles and Other Prey: A Vietnam Experience in Prose and Poetry.* N.p.:Volunteer Publications, 1989.

William Eastlake. *The Bamboo Bed.* New York: Simon & Schuster, 1969.

W. D. Ehrhart, ed. *Carrying the Darkness: The Poetry of the Vietnam War.* Lubbock, Tx.: Texas Tech University Press, 1989.

Graham Greene. *The Quiet American.* 1955; reprint, New York: Penguin Classics, 2004.

Norman Mailer. *Armies of the Night.* 1968; reprint, New York: Plume, 1995. The Pulitzer Prize–winning book is a novelized account of the protest march on the Pentagon in 1967.

David Maraniss. *They Marched into Sunlight: War and Peace/Vietnam and America/October 1967.* New York: Simon & Schuster, 2002.

Harold G. Moore and Joseph L. Galloway. *We Were Soldiers Once . . . and Young.* 1992; reprint, New York: Presidio Press, 2004.

Robin Moore. *The Green Berets.* 1965; reprint, New York: St. Martin's, 2002.

Tim O'Brien. *The Things They Carried.* 1970; reprint, New York: Penguin, 1991.

Tim O'Brien. *If I Die in a Combat Zone, Box Me Up and Ship Me Home.* 1973; reprint, New York: Dell, 1983.

Geoffrey Stamm. *Atrocities: Vietnam Poetry.* Hiram, Ohio: Hiram Poetry Review, 1989.

Robert Stone. *Dog Soldiers.* 1974; reprint, New York: Penguin USA, 1989.

Larry Weinberg. *War Zone.* New York: Bantam, 1985. (young adult fiction)

Theater

Megan Terry. *Viet-Rock.* 1966; reprinted in *Plays by Megan Terry* (New York: Broadway Play Publishers, 1999).

Emily Mann. *Still Life.* 1981; reprinted in Emily Mann, *Testimonies: Four Plays* (New York: Theatre Communications Group, 1997).

John DiFusco (conception). *Tracers.* 1983; actor's edition available through Dramatists Play Service (www.dramatists.com).

Claude-Michel Schönberg and Alain Boubli (lyrics by Alain Boubli and Richard Maltby). *Miss Saigon.* 1989; paperback ed., Milwaukee, Wis.: Hal Leonard Corporation, 1993. The studio cast recording of this long-running Broadway musical was issued by Angel Records in 1995.

Paris Barclay. *One Red Flower: Letters from Nam.* 2004; based on letters collected in Bernard Edelman, ed., *Dear America: Letters Home from Viet Nam* (1985; reprint, New York: Norton, 2002).

Nora M. Alter. *Vietnam Protest Theatre: The Television War on Stage.* Bloomington, Ind.: Indiana University Press, 1996.

Movies

The Green Berets (1968), directed by Ray Kellogg. Starring John Wayne, this early Vietnam film focuses on guerilla warfare.

Coming Home (1978), directed by Hal Ashby. Set in 1968 and starring Jane Fonda and Jon Voigt, the movie deals with a soldier's life after his return from the war.

The Deer Hunter (1978), directed by Michael Cimino. The film, based on the 1978 book by E. M. Corder, tracks a group of steelworker pals through the war.

Apocalypse Now (1979), directed by Francis Ford Coppola. Though set in Vietnam, the film is loosely based on Joseph Conrad's 1902 novel *Heart of Darkness.*

Platoon (1986), directed by Oliver Stone. This psychological drama concerns a group of soldiers on patrol in the jungles of Vietnam.

Full Metal Jacket (1987), directed by Stanley Kubrick. Based on Gustav Hasford's 1980 novel *The Short Timers,* the movie focuses on a group of marines during basic training and then in Vietnam during the Tet Offensive.

Good Morning Vietnam (1987), directed by Barry Levinson. Starring Robin Williams, the film is based on the life of Adrian Cronauer, a disk jockey on military radio in Vietnam during the mid-1960s.

The Hanoi Hilton (1987), directed by Lionel Chetwynd. The movie tells the story of POWs in North Vietnam's Hoa Lo Prison.

Born on the Fourth of July (1989), directed by Oliver Stone. Based on the true story of Ron Kovic (played by Tom Cruise in an early starring role), the movie is about a soldier during his tour of duty in Vietnam and after his return home.

Casualties of War (1989), directed by Brian DePalma. The true story of a squadron of soldiers and the moral dilemmas they faced, the film is based on the 1969 book by Daniel Lang.

We Were Soldiers (2002), directed by Randall Wallace. The movie is based on the book *We Were Soldiers Once . . . and Young,* by Lt. Gen. Harold G. Moore.

Television

Tour of Duty (1987–1990); dramatic series.

China Beach (1988–1991); comedy series.

Dear America: Letters Home from Viet Nam (1987), directed by Bill Couturié. This HBO movie was based on the 1985 book by Bernard Edelman.

"Two Days in October" (2005), directed by Robert Kenner. This episode of the PBS series *The American Experience* (www.pbs.org/wgbh/amex/twodays/) was based on the book *They Marched into Sunlight,* by David Maraniss.

Music

The Vietnam War inspired a wave of protest music, ranging from folksinger Buffy Sainte-Marie's "Universal Soldier" through John Lennon's "Give Peace a Chance" (1969) and "Imagine" (1971). Other well-known antiwar songs of the period include, to name just a few, "Eve of Destruction," by Barry McGuire (1965); "Fortunate Son," by Creedence Clearwater Revival (1968); and "The I-Feel-Like-I'm-Fixin'-to-Die Rag," by Country Joe and the Fish (1967). The last of these was especially popular among soldiers stationed in Vietnam, as was Eric Burdon and the Animals' "We Gotta Get Out of this Place" (1965). Not all the popular music of the period took issue with the war, however; songs like Barry Sadler's "The Ballad of the Green Berets" (a number-one hit in 1966) and patriotic songs by country artists such as Merle Haggard and Dave Dudley were also chart-toppers. Resources on Vietnam-era music include these:

Lee Andresen. *Battle Notes: Music of the Vietnam War.* Superior, Wis.: Savage Press, 2002.

Barbara Dane and Irwin Silber. eds. *The Vietnam Songbook: More than 100 Songs from the American and International Protest Movements and Fighting Songs of the Vietnamese People.* N.p: The Guardian, 1969.

Visual Arts

In 1981, the National Vietnam Veterans Art Museum was founded in Chicago. Its exhibits feature visual art about Vietnam as well as later U.S. wars. Visit its Web site at www.nvvam.org/aboutus/index.htm.

Lucy Lippard. *A Different War: Vietnam in Art*. Bellingham, Wash.: Whatcom Museum of History and Art, 1990.

GULF WAR

Fiction, Memoirs, and Poetry

Tom Clancy, with Chuck Horner. *Every Man a Tiger*. New York: Putnam Adult, 1999.

Terrence D. Haynes. *Desert Norm: A Journal/Novel About the Gulf War*. Lincoln, Neb.: Writers Club Press (iUniverse), 2002.

G. Richard Holt. *The Rising Storm: A Novel About the Persian Gulf War*. Houston: Larksdale Press, 1993.

Andy McNab. *Bravo Two Zero*. N.p.: Corgi Adult, 2005.

Thomas E. Ricks. *A Soldier's Duty: A Novel*. New York: Random House, 2002.

Charles Sheehan-Miles. *Prayer at Rumayla*. Philadelphia: Xlibris, 2001.

William Heyen. *Ribbons: The Gulf War—A Poem*. St. Louis: Time Being Books, 1991.

Movies

The Finest Hour (1991), directed by Shimon Dotan. The film tells the story of two men who become best friends while training to become Navy SEALs.

Courage under Fire (1996), directed by Edward Zwick. The movie stars Meg Ryan as Capt. Karen Emma Walden, the first woman to receive a Medal of Honor (posthumously).

Three Kings (1999), directed by David O. Russell. The film, starring George Clooney, is a fictional tale of American soldiers looking for stolen Kuwaiti bullion in Iraq just after the Gulf War.

Lessons of Darkness (German title: *Lektionen in Finsternis*; 2002), directed by Werner Herzog. This documentary relates the story of the oilfield fires in Kuwait.

The Manchurian Candidate (2004), directed by Jonathan Demme. This remake of the 1962 movie by John Frankenheimer uses the Persian Gulf War of 1991, instead of the Korean War, as its backstory.

Jarhead (2005), directed by Sam Mendes. Starring Jake Gyllenhaal, the film is an adaptation of Anthony Swofford's 2001 book *Jarhead: A Marine's Chronicle of the Gulf War and other Battles*.

Television

The One That Got Away (1996), directed by Paul Greengrass. This made-for-TV movie was based on Chris Ryan's 1998 book *The One That Got Away: My SAS Mission behind Enemy Lines*.

Bravo Two Zero (1998), directed by Tom Clegg. Also made for TV, the film is based on the book by Andy McNab.

Live From Baghdad (2002), directed by Mick Jackson. This HBO film tells the story of CNN reporters in Iraq during the war.

Music

Being so brief, the Gulf War inspired relatively little popular music. Two songs of the era that did draw their inspiration from the conflict are "KYEO," by Fugazi, from the 1991 album *Steady Diet of Nothing*, and "Gulf War Song," by Moxy Fruvous, from the 1994 album *Bargainville*.

Visual Arts

The Gulf War was the first conflict to inspire creators of a brand-new medium: video games. Among the games based on Gulf War themes are *Super Battletank: War in the Gulf* (Majesco, 1992); *Gulf War: Operation Desert Hammer* (Gamespot, 1999); *Conflict: Desert Storm* (MobyGames, 2002); and *Conflict: Desert Storm 2 (Back to Baghdad)* (MobyGames, 2003).

AFGHANISTAN AND IRAQ WARS

Memoirs and Poetry

Rick Bragg. *I Am a Soldier, Too: The Jessica Lynch Story*. New York: Knopf, 2003.

Oliver North and Sara Horn. *A Greater Freedom: Stories of Faith from Operation Iraqi Freedom*. Nashville, Tenn.: B&H Publishing Group, 2004.

Sam Hamill, ed. *Poets Against the War*. New York: Thunder's Mouth Press, 2003.

Theater

Tim Robbins. *Embedded*. 2004. The satirical play portrays a U.S. invasion of a fictional nation called Gomorrah.

Sean Huze. *The Sand Storm: Stories from the Front*. 2005. Playwright Huze is an Iraq War veteran.

Sean Huze. *The Wolf*. 2007.

Simon Levy. *What I Heard about Iraq (A Cry for Five Voices)*. 2004 (based on a prose poem by Eliot Weinberger).

Richard Norton-Taylor. *Called to Account: The Indictment of Anthony Charles Lynton Blair for the Crime of Aggression Against Iraq*. London: Oberon Books, 2007. This British antiwar play presents a mock war-crimes trial of then–prime minister Tony Blair.

Movies

Fire over Afghanistan (2003), directed by Terence H. Winkless. The story relates what happens after a Black Hawk helicopter pilot is shot down in Afghanistan.

American Soldiers (2005), directed by Sidney J. Furie. The film is about an ambush of a routine U.S. patrol in Iraq.

Home of the Brave (2006), directed by Irwin Winkler. The movie follows three soldiers after their return from Iraq.

G.I. Jesus (2007), directed by Carl Colpaert. The film portrays a Mexican Marine promised U.S. citizenship in exchange for service.

Redacted (2007), directed by Brian DePalma. This controversial movie, a followup to DePalma's film about Vietnam, *Casualties of War*, examines atrocities committed by U.S. soldiers in Iraq.

The Situation (2007), directed by Philip Haas. A love triangle is played out against the backdrop of the Iraq War in this film.

Television

Last Letters Home: Voices of American Troops from the Battlefields of Iraq (2004), directed by Bill Couturié. Families of men and women killed in action read their loved ones' final letters in this HBO documentary.

Over There (2005), created by Steven Bochco and Chris Gerolmo; dramatic series.

Baghdad ER (2006), directed by Jon Alpert and Matthew O'Neill. This HBO documentary reveals the grueling conditions under which doctors work in a military hospital in Baghdad.

Alive Day Memories (2007), executive producer James Gandolfini. Gandolfini interviews wounded Iraq veterans in this HBO documentary.

America at a Crossroads (2007). This PBS documentary series examines American involvement in Afghanistan and Iraq, among other, related topics.

Music

The Iraq War has inspired a great deal of popular music, with musicians taking one or the other side in the intense debate about the war's legitimacy. Songs supporting the war have included Darryl Worley's "Have You Forgotten?" (2003) and Clint Black's "I Raq and Roll." Staking out a politically neutral territory, Bruce Springsteen's album *The Rising* (2002), focused instead on broad themes of tragedy and loss. Musical protests include Willie Nelson's song "Whatever Happened to Peace on Earth?" (2003), R.E.M.'s "The Final Straw," the Beastie Boys' "In a World Gone Mad," Steve Earle's "The Revolution Starts Now," and Neil Young's album *Living with War* (2007).

Visual Arts

Richard Johnson and Steve Siedel. *Portraits of War*. Detroit: Detroit Free Press, 2003.

Steve Mumford. *Baghdad Journal: An Artist in Occupied Iraq*. Montreal: Drawn and Quarterly, 2005.

GENERAL REFERENCES

Literature and History

Walter Cronkite and Robert Hedin, eds. *Old Glory: American War Poems from the Revolutionary War to the War on Terrorism*. New York: Persea Books, 2004.

Philip K. Jason and Mark A. Graves, eds. *Encyclopedia of American War Literature*. Westport, Conn.: Greenwood, 2000.

Jon E. Lewis, ed. *The Mammoth Book of War Diaries and Letters: Life on the Battlefield in the Words of the Ordinary Soldier*. New York: Carroll & Graf, 1999.

David H. Lowenherz. *The 50 Greatest Letters from American Wars*. New York: Crown, 2002.

Online History Resources

http://userpages.aug.com/captbarb/lives.html. The site provides information on American women who gave their lives in service to their country.

www.pbs.org/wgbh/amex/warletters. The Web site is devoted to an episode of the PBS series *The American Experience* that focused on soldiers' letters from the battlefield.

www1.va.gov/opa/fact/amwars.asp. This Veterans Department Web site provides statistical information on all of the wars America has fought.

Theater

Eric Bentley. *Theatre of War*. New York: Viking, 1972.

Movies

Robert Eberwein, ed. *The War Film.* New Brunswick, N.J.: Rutgers University Press, 2004.

J. David Slocum. *Hollywood and War: The Film Reader.* New York: Routledge, 2006.

Music

Olivia Bailey. *Songs and Music that Inspired Courage during Wartime.* Caldwell, Idaho: Caxton, 2004.

Charles K. Wolfe and James E. Akeson. *Country Music Goes to War.* Lexington, Ky.: University Press of Kentucky, 2005.

Online Music Resources

www.lacarte.org/songs/anti-war/. This site allows you to research antiwar songs by dozens of artists.

www.soldierssongs.com. This Web site includes essays and a study guide to soldiers' songs from the Civil War on.

Visual Arts

A. D. Harvey. *A Muse of Fire: Literature, Art and War.* London: Hambledon & London, 2003.

ABOUT THE EXHIBITION

THE AMERICAN SOLDIER From the Civil War to the War in Iraq: *A Photographic Tribute* is the first exhibition of its kind ever mounted. The idea for the exhibit dates to 1995, when curator Cyma Rubin was inspired by a photograph of a World War II G.I. that appeared on the cover of the *New York Times Magazine.* It was not until 2004, however, that she began collecting the photographs that appear in the show. In examining more than 4,000 photographs covering nearly 150 years of American military history, Ms. Rubin and her staff decided to focus on the real lives of American soldiers—army troops and Marines—through the nine major wars America has fought since 1861. They decided, too, to choose photographs—many of them not widely seen before—that would tell the story of American soldiers' camaraderie, courage, humor, and sacrifice.

The 116 photographs ultimately chosen for the exhibition show how America's wars have looked "on the ground"—through the eyes of the men (and, in recent years, women) who have fought them, and through the lenses of the photographers who have bravely accompanied America's combat forces into battle. As the viewer follows the American soldier from the Civil War through the War in Iraq, it becomes obvious that some things have changed: uniforms, weaponry, medical care, communications. What is even more obvious, though, is how much remains constant: the youthful faces, the horror of battle, the weary endurance of summer heat and winter cold, the suffering—these are all the same.

We Americans fervently support our troops, but for those of us at home, the sacrifice of our fighting men and women is too often an abstraction. THE AMERICAN SOLDIER provides an up-close view of their service, honoring those who have risked—and sometimes given—their lives for our safety and protection. The exhibition's purpose is both commemorative and educational, giving children and young adults a vivid sense of just how much today's soldiers and their predecessors have given us. And it likewise celebrates the contributions made by the photojournalists—some famous, some anonymous—who have also risked danger at the front lines, and without whose work we could not experience these moments of history.